ASHE Higher Education Report: Volume 31, Number 1
Adrianna J. Kezar, Kelly Ward, Lisa E. Wolf-Wendel, Series Editors

The Challenge of Diversity

Involvement or Alienation in the Academy?

Daryl G. Smith and Lisa E. Wolf-Wendel

New edition—originally
released in 1989

The Challenge of Diversity: Involvement or Alienation in the Academy?

Daryl G. Smith and Lisa E. Wolf-Wendel

ASHE Higher Education Report: Volume 31, Number 1

Adrianna J. Kezar, Kelly Ward, Lisa E. Wolf-Wendel, Series Editors

ISSN 1551-6970   electronic ISSN 1554-6306   ISBN 0-7879-8122-2

The ASHE Higher Education Report is part of the Jossey-Bass Higher and Adult
Education Series and is published six times a year by Wiley Subscription Services,
Inc., A Wiley Company, at Jossey-Bass, 989 Market Street, San Francisco, Califor-
nia 94103-1741.

For subscription information, see the Back Issue/Subscription Order Form
in the back of this volume.

CALL FOR PROPOSALS: Prospective authors are strongly encouraged to contact
Kelly Ward (kaward@wsu.edu) or Lisa Wolf-Wendel (lwolf@ku.edu). See "About
the ASHE Higher Education Report Series" in the back of this volume.

Visit the Jossey-Bass Web site at **www.josseybass.com.**

Printed in the United States of America on acid-free recycled paper.

Advisory Board

The ASHE Higher Education Report Series is sponsored by the Association for the Study of Higher Education (ASHE), which provides an editorial advisory board of ASHE members.

Contents

New Foreword

It gives me great pleasure that Daryl G. Smith agreed to work with me to write a new introduction to her 1989 monograph and to re-release it. We initially thought that we might engage in a more extensive update of the monograph, but after reading the original we both agreed that relatively little of substance had changed since 1989 and that the monograph still "had legs." As a result, the following monograph is untouched.

Daryl G. Smith's monograph is responsible for framing how many contemporary scholars and administrators in higher education think about diversity today. The original text points out that diversity in higher education extends beyond merely providing access to historically underrepresented groups. Daryl eloquently makes the case that institutions of higher education must intentionally transform themselves to become places that meet the imperative of diversity.

This monograph, in its original form, is still relevant and has important lessons for practitioners and scholars alike. I hope that the re-release of this monograph provides an impetus for further action in our progress towards making higher education more accessible and equitable.

Lisa E. Wolf-Wendel
Series Editor

New Introduction

In 1989, when *The Challenge of Diversity* was first published, the monograph made the case that engaging the changing demographics of the country meant reframing diversity to focus on the capacity of institutions to educate and involve increasingly diverse student populations. Looking at research at the time, the monograph pointed to patterns of alienation, not involvement, and suggested that reframing diversity issues to look at institutional effectiveness was critical. Further, the book argued that providing high quality higher education to all potential students had civic, economic, and political significance for society.

Rereading the manuscript is sobering. As the demographics of the student body have indeed changed, many of the issues addressed have remained. Not only are access and success of underrepresented populations (African American, Latino, and Native American students) still challenges for higher education; but, many of the challenges with the curriculum, institutional practice, climate, and hiring remain unresolved. At the same time, the context for diversity today has changed. If in 1989, the monograph was asserting that higher education had little capacity to educate students who were considered nontraditional at the time, today, one could easily demonstrate that the nontraditional students (especially in relationship to older students, women, and part-time students) are now the traditional students. (See New Table 1.) Adding to the core of unmet challenges is the growing diversity within racial and ethnic groups, increasing numbers of multiracial students and students from Southeast Asia, and deep growth in religious pluralism on campus. Indeed, while higher education has changed profoundly, it is also clear that our institutions have not yet

NEW TABLE 1

Higher Education Enrollments by Age, Gender, and Attendance Status, 1995 and 2000

	1995		2000	
	No.	*Percent*	*No.*	*Percent*
Total	14,262	—	15,312	61
14–24 years	8,158	57	9,338	61
25 years and older	6,103	43	5,974	39
Men	6,372	45	6,722	44
Women	7,907	55	8,591	56
Full time	8,129	57	9,010	59
Part time	6,133	43	6,303	41

SOURCE: Center for Education Statistics, 2002.

developed the capacity to successfully educate the diversity of students present on our campuses today. In addition, we are experiencing a profound backlash to some diversity initiatives that have the potential to negatively affect how higher education responds to diversity. There are also other societal factors and indicators that lead one to believe that higher education will have to become more proactive in responding favorably to diversity. As a result of these factors, if the monograph were published now, we would change the name from *The Challenge of Diversity* to *The Imperative of Diversity.*

The Context for Diversity Outside of Higher Education

Since 1989, there have been several legal and political challenges to affirmative action that have created a more hostile environment for making progress in diversifying the student body as well as faculty and staff. For example, in 1995, the University of California Board of Regents implemented a policy that eliminated the use of race and ethnicity in admissions. A year later, California voters approved Proposition 209, which amended the state constitution to ban "race-conscious admissions decisions" in the state's public education system. In 1996 the Fifth Circuit Court ordered Texas to eliminate all "race-conscious affirmative action" in university admissions decisions (*Hopwood* v. *Texas*). In Florida, Governor Bush had the State Board of Education ban "consideration of race in admissions decisions" for the state's higher education institutions. The Florida postsecondary system, however, was allowed to consider race and ethnicity in awarding scholarships and other financial aid, conducting outreach, and developing pre-college summer programs. In 2003 the United States Supreme Court ruled that the University of Michigan could continue to use race in admissions decisions under a "narrowly tailored" plan because there was a "a compelling interest in obtaining the educational benefits that flow from a diverse student body which is not prohibited by the Equal Protection Clause of the 14th Amendment." A number of the Supreme Court Justices wrote dissenting opinions and even Justice O'Connor, who supported the use of race in admissions, suggested that the use of race/ethnicity in college admissions should be a temporary remedy until such time that equity of access has been achieved. Nonetheless, this decision was important for its acknowledgment of the significance of race in the context of the educational mission and societal role of higher education. Moreover, it resulted in a significant increase in research, especially social science research, on the impact and benefits of diversity (Bowen and Bok, 1998; Chang and Associates, 1999).

Since the 1980s, changes in federal and state financial aid policies combined with increasing tuition have also made it increasingly difficult for low-income students (a high percentage of whom are from underrepresented racial/ethnic groups) to gain access to higher education. The shift from grants to loans has also made higher education beyond the reach of many low-income students. These factors have created a situation where the gap in college attendance rates between low and high-income students has widened, even controlling for academic preparation (National Center for Public Policy and Higher Education, 2003).

Since 1989, there have also been a series of forces that are elevating diversity to prominence and urgency. The first such force is changing demography. While demographic changes were predicted in the 1989 monograph, the demographic shifts are now a reality, making it impossible to pretend that diversity isn't important. Indeed, we are in the midst of the largest pattern of immigration our country has ever experienced, which has profound implications for everything we do. We see demographic changes throughout the country—in places like Texas and California, for example "minorities" are now the majority. In other regions of the country—including the Midwest and Northeast, there is a much larger proportion of historically underrepresented groups than ever before (WICHE, 2004). Such demographic changes underscore the importance of higher education responding positively to diversity. Further, there have been some interesting opinion poll data recently collected for the Ford Foundation (1998) that demonstrates that over 90 percent of the public believes diversity is important and that American higher education ought to be addressing these issues on their campuses.

Another pressure for higher education to consider issues of diversity comes from the professional and business communities that are increasingly recognizing how important it is to serve diverse communities and to make sure that members of society have the competence to engage diversity. Significantly, General Motors and a consortium of Fortune 500 companies wrote an amicus brief in support of the University of Michigan in their 2003 Affirmative Action case. The brief stated that "racial and ethnic diversity in institutions of higher education is vital to *amici's* efforts to hire and maintain a diverse workforce, and to employ individuals of all backgrounds who have been educated in a diverse environment. Such a talented workforce is important to *amici's* continued success in the global marketplace." It is clear that businesses want to hire individuals who know how to work in diverse settings and who are competent in working with diversity. Indeed, these sectors are spending millions of dollars to train employees on how to work with diverse communities. Many of these sectors are expecting higher education to do its share to educate future workers about how to work in diverse settings and with diverse individuals (Bikson, 1996; Carnevale, 1999; Cox, 1993; Loden and Rosener, 1991; Morrison, 1992).

The imperative of diversity has significant global dimensions as well. Conversations linking diversity, democracy, and higher education have occurred in countries throughout the world, recognizing that democracies cannot be viable unless diversity is engaged. Central to the success of this effort will be the role of higher education and its ability to educate the diversity that exists within any nation (Beckham, 2000; Cloete and Associates, 1997; Cross and

Associates, 1999). In addition, many nations are struggling to address past inequities. Most nations have not developed the capacity to engage the legacy and history of past injustices (Barkan, 2000). This history along with continuing injustice in the present dramatically impacts contemporary conversations throughout the world. Issues of diversity are central to the success of political structures and the viability of nations across the world. Furthermore, we see countries around the world struggling with how to work with the sovereignty of indigenous groups and the preservation of cultures and languages across the world. For the United States, each of these issues has significance for our credibility as a democratic country (Cuarasci and Associates, 1997; Musil and Associates, 1999).

It is in connection to these external and institutional factors that colleges and universities find themselves dealing with diversity. Before moving forward, it is helpful to define what is meant by diversity. Since the publication of the original monograph, Daryl Smith designed a framework to assist practitioners and researchers in thinking about the components of diversity. Rather than viewing diversity as a laundry list of activities or identities, this framework conceptualizes diversity in higher education as four distinct but interrelated dimensions focusing on the institution: access and success, campus climate and intergroup relations, education and scholarship, and institutional viability and vitality. Each of these dimensions is discussed separately.

Access and Success

The first dimension, access and success, has been concerned with the inclusion and success of historically underrepresented groups—African Americans, Latinos, and Native Americans. It focuses on both social justice and education in that it seeks to redress historical disadvantages experienced by these groups. Diversity efforts began in this dimension in the mid 1960s and were focused primarily on providing access to historically underrepresented groups identified by race, ethnicity, and gender. The focus has been on student representation on campus, representation in relation to some larger population, and graduation/completion rates.

Since 1989, the data on access and success have shown some improvement but are still not at equitable levels. Progress in this domain is becoming more

NEW TABLE 2
Higher Education Enrollment Percentages by Racial or Ethnic Group, 1976 to 2000

	European Americans	African Americans	Latinos	Asian Americans	Native Americans	International
1976	82.6%	9.4%	3.5%	1.8%	.7%	2.0%
1980	81.3%	9.2%	3.9%	2.4%	.7%	2.5%
1990	77.6%	9.1%	5.7%	4.1%	.7%	2.8%
1995	72.3%	10.3%	7.7%	5.6%	.9%	3.2%
2000	68.3%	11.3%	9.6%	6.4%	1.0%	3.4%

urgent over time. From a racial/ethnic demographic perspective, the current status of enrollment demonstrates that higher education is more diverse today than ever before (see New Table 2). The changing demographics predicted earlier are now a reality, whereas for many campuses the demographic shift had once been just a projection. Indeed, the increasing diversity of the undergraduate population can lead an institution to think it is "diverse" and thus can ignore issues like the continuing achievement gaps on campus. When we look at access to higher education what we see is that the proportion of Latino students has increased, though they are still underrepresented in relationship to their numbers in the population. Access to higher education by Asian Americans and African Americans has also increased steadily. Native Americans remain underrepresented. While access has improved for African Americans and Latinos, however, it is important to note that they are overrepresented within two-year colleges and among less selective four year institutions (see New Tables 3 and 4) (National Center for Education Statistics, 2002).

Another way to look at access to higher education is to look at the percentage of high school graduates who enroll in college by race/ethnicity. Data suggest that there are still important racial/ethnic disparities present. Overall, in 2002, 65.2 percent of the 2001–2002 high school graduates enrolled in college. For whites, the college continuation rate in 2002 was 69.1 percent. For African Americans the percentage was 58.7 percent and for Latinos the percentage was 53.5 percent. The percentage for Asian Americans was 61.2 percent (Mortenson, 2003a). Interestingly, between 1979 and 1986, the

NEW TABLE 3
Higher Education Enrollment Percentages at Four-Year Institutions by Racial/Ethnic Group, 1976 to 2000

	European Americans	African Americans	Latinos	Asian Americans	Native Americans	International
1976	84.4%	8.5%	2.4%	1.7%	.5%	2.5%
1980	82.9%	8.4%	2.9%	2.1%	.5%	3.2%
1990	78.9%	8.4%	4.2%	4.2%	.6%	3.8%
1995	74.3%	9.7%	5.5%	5.5%	.7%	4.2%
2000	71.1%	10.6%	6.6%	6.2%	.8%	4.7%

NEW TABLE 4
Higher Education Enrollment Percentages at Two-Year Institutions by Racial/Ethnic Group, 1976 to 2000

	European Americans	African Americans	Latinos	Asian Americans	Native Americans	International
1976	79.3%	11.1%	5.4%	2.0%	1.1%	1.1%
1980	78.7%	10.4%	5.6%	2.8%	1.0%	1.4%
1990	75.5%	10.0%	8.1%	4.1%	1.0%	1.3%
1995	69.1%	11.3%	11.1%	5.7%	1.2%	1.6%
2000	64.0%	12.4%	14.2%	6.8%	1.3%	1.5%

percentage of African Americans who continued from high school to college declined from 45.4 to 36.5 percent (despite increases in the African American high school graduation rates during this same period). Since that time period (1986 to 2002), African Americans have improved their college continuation rates though they still lag behind the population. The college continuation rate for Latinos has remained flat since 1976, hovering between 52 and 53 percent. Data suggest that since 1979, Latinos have fallen behind the population in terms of their continuation rate to college (Mortenson, 2003a).

College graduation rates by race/ethnicity remain an urgent concern. While census data show some progress, institutional graduation rates suggest that significant gaps remain. This is another area that demonstrates some, though not complete, progress since the 1989 monograph was published. Specifically, in 2002, 29.3 percent of the proportion of 25 to 29 year olds in the United States population had completed four or more years of college. In 1980 that figure was 22.5 percent and in 1990 that figure was 23.2 percent. For whites, the percentage of individuals 25 to 29 with four years of college was 35.9 percent in 2002. For African Americans, 18 percent had completed 4 or more years of college. In contrast, the rate was 8.9 percent for Latinos. The long-term trend demonstrates improvements over time for all racial/ethnic groups—though the growth was lowest for Latinos (who increased 3.2 percent from 1974 to 2002). African Americans increased 10.1 percent and whites increased 13.9 percent during the same period (Mortenson, 2003b).

Since 1989, we have also seen some changes in the ways researchers and institutions of higher education have examined issues of access and success. Early research focused on exploring why historically underrepresented students didn't come to higher education and/or why they weren't successful when they arrived. In other words, past research focused on explaining failure by examining what was wrong with the students and their academic preparation. In contrast, research today focuses more on examining what institutions of higher education are doing to address access and success—the focus is more often on the institution and its success or failures rather than on the student (Hurtado and Associates, 1998; Rendon and Hope, 1996; Moses, 1999; Smith, 1995). Today we recognize the institution's responsibility in providing environments where diverse students can achieve success. Graduation and persistence data are very important measures of institutional success. Indeed, we are even raising the bar by asking not just whether historically underrepresented students are graduating but examining the extent to which they are thriving, are engaged in the academic enterprise, are graduating with honors, are graduating in math, science and engineering fields, etc. (Hurtado, 1994; Maton and Hrabowski, 2004). Work has continued significantly at looking at the conditions for success and new ways to think about factors influencing success, including the important work of such scholars as Gandara (1999), Steele (1997), and Treisman (1992).

The very dynamic nature of diversity is exemplified by the way we are also faced with new questions and the need for new ways to look at access and success. For example, since 1989 we have seen an increasing need to disaggregate data from different groups. Research shows that not all Latinos are alike—with some groups like the Cuban Americans fairing quite well in higher education while others like Mexican Americans fairing less well. Further, within the Asian American population, diversity is very great and within that group there are huge issues of underrepresentation. Because higher education has tended to think of Asian Americans as the model majority, we have ignored the fact that some subgroups, including the Filipinos, Hmong, and Laotians, for example, are not well represented within the college-going population. Aggregation of groups together is one way of analyzing data and creating large enough groups to advocate for change; nonetheless there is a great need to disaggregate results to look at differences within groups (Espiritu, 1997; Hune and Chan, 1997; Nakanishi and Nishida, 1995). While group size often determines the level of analysis, it has also become urgent to look at American Indian students, faculty, and experiences more closely. Paradoxically, the smaller size of this highly underrepresented group often results in being omitted in research studies on access and success.

Further, we now recognize that when looking at access to higher education it is increasingly important to look at socioeconomic status as well as race and ethnicity. Class is not just a function of access to financial aid, it is also a matter of cultural and social capital and the intersection between class and race is terribly important (Borrego, 2003; McDonough, 1997; Zandy, 2001). Research demonstrates that family income and parental education largely determines whether a child will be a college graduate. Specifically, research shows that in 2002 only 6 percent of individuals from the bottom quartile of family income (below $35,000) earned a bachelor's degree by age 24. The percentage increases to 12.7 percent for those in the second income quartile (between $35,000 and $61,000) and increases to 26.8 percent for those in the third income quartile ($61,000 to $90,000). Fifty-one percent of those in the highest income quartile earned an undergraduate degree by age 24. Different racial/ethnic groups have different family income profiles. Specifically, in 2002, within the bottom quartile 61 percent of dependent 18 to 24 year olds were minorities, 38.3 percent of the second quartile were minorities, 22.7 percent of the third quartile were minorities, and 17.8 percent of the top quartile were minorities (Mortenson, 2004).

The new census data acknowledges the vast growing number of Americans who are multiracial. The growth in the number of Americans from mixed backgrounds, many of whom are coming to colleges and universities, challenge our binary ways of thinking about minority and majority status. Many people are neither this nor that but are, instead, some combination of both this and that racial/ethnic background. This recognition of multiethnic backgrounds calls for the need for us to think differently about how we categorize people.

One of the important areas related to access that still requires more attention has to do with how institutions of higher education determine who should have access. Currently, as we have done for a long time, higher education relies quite heavily on standardized testing to identify who will be successful in higher education. Standardized tests determine access to the most elite institutions as well as access to scholarships and grants. We know that such tests under-predict the potential of students from diverse backgrounds, but we seem incapable of identifying talent in other ways. How to identify talent and discern what student characteristics are most predictive of postsecondary success will continue to be a question in search of an answer (Sedlacek, 2004).

Climate and Intergroup Relations

The second dimension of diversity is climate and intergroup relationships. Climate is an important part of the diversity equation in that it asks how institutions of higher education are involving, including, and engaging students from diverse backgrounds. When we talk about institutional climate, the definition of diversity broadens from including historically underrepresented groups to also including difference based on sexual orientation, religion, physical ability, and so forth. Of particular importance today seems to be the climate for gay, lesbian, and transgender students as well as the climate for Muslim students after 9/11 (Herek and Capitano, 1996; Tierney, 1993).

Twenty years ago we thought that campus climate was the key issue. Today, we know that it is a much more complicated construct than we had initially believed. For example, researchers today find it difficult to detect whether women students are experiencing a chilly climate. They also haven't found evidence of behaviors that lead to a chilly climate (Whitt and Associates, 1998). Nonetheless, we know that men and women experience the academic environment differently and that women still seem to be underperforming in many domains within higher education. Further we know that even though undergraduates don't perceive a chilly climate, graduate students and faculty members continue to report experiencing micro-inequities that make them feel unwelcome in higher education (Turner and Myers, 2000). In the old model, we thought about the chilly climate as being a product of individual behavior—now we think of it as an environment that does not feel fully welcoming, the cause of which may be a whole range of things that are hard to pinpoint. This leads us to the conclusion that while climate is a useful indicator of how different groups perceive the institution, it need not be a function of specific behaviors.

In the 1989 monograph, the importance of how issues are framed was a central perspective. The importance of framing is best exemplified today by the issue of self-segregation. As campuses have become more diverse, many institutional leaders express concern about self-segregation—that is, the apparent tendency for students of color to stay together. By framing this issue as a problem caused by students of color, institutions once again suggest that the issue is not an institutional one. Indeed, research suggests that if there is self-segregation on campuses, it is mostly white students who have little contact with others, rather than the reverse (Antonio, 2001; Smith and Associates, 1997; Tatum, 1997).

New research also suggests that the campus experience must be examined from the perspective of multiple groups and that disaggregation of data is increasingly important. In particular, emphasis needs to be placed on examining diversity within communities as well as on intergroup relationships across communities of color and not just concerned with interactions with whites. Indeed, as campuses become more diverse, you see a greater need to focus on intergroup and intragroup relationships—the extent to which groups do and don't work together. Research in social psychology suggests that there are certain conditions that must be in place in order for individuals of different groups to work together. Specifically, we know that institutions need to bring diverse people together in ways that emphasize equality of status—rather than in ways that emphasize existing power structures. Working together across difference also requires a commitment to the end goal and its importance. Lastly, we know that intergroup relationships are enhanced when there is a critical mass of people from different groups so that people can be seen as individuals rather than as token members of a group (Brewer, 2000; Pettigrew and Tropp, 2000).

Education and Scholarship

The third dimension of diversity is called education and scholarship—factors that are central to the core of higher education. In this dimension, institutions ask themselves how we are preparing our students to work in diverse communities and to work with people who are different from us. Research shows that when students are exposed to diverse perspectives through interaction with diverse others and through the curriculum they develop more complex and critical thinking skills and actually learn more. Further, research shows that exposing students to multiple points of view on issues that matter and that have some emotional significance leads to positive outcomes for all students regardless of the students' background characteristics (Gurin, Dey, Hurtado, and Gurin, 2002; Gudeman, 2000; Marin, 2000; Maruyama and Moreno, 2000; Schoem and Associates, 1993). Research findings also demonstrate that a diverse curriculum leads to increased commitment to civic engagement, democratic outcomes, community participation during and after college, and the likelihood of having diverse friendships (Antonio, 2001; Hurtado and Associates, 2002).

Interestingly, one of the significant research findings that has emerged from the research over the past few years is that perceiving that the institution is committed to diversity makes a big difference in terms of student outcomes (Hurtado, 1996; Smith and Associates, 1997; Orfield, 2001). Specifically, research on the effects of diversity (interactional and curricular) was influential for students from all racial/ethnic groups and lead to students believing they can influence the political structure, influence social values, help others in difficulty, be involved in programs to clean the environment, and participate in community action programs. Campus diversity initiatives also lead to improved cultural awareness and appreciation, and increased acceptance of persons from different races or cultures. Lastly, diversity initiatives have also led to improved learning outcomes (intellectual engagement, self-assessed academic skills). This new body of research also reveals the continuing need to look at design and implementation of initiatives because the results of these efforts, while beneficial to whites most clearly, may not be as powerful for others (Chang, Astin, and Kim, 2004).

One of the most important areas of recent emphasis within the domain of education and scholarship has to do with a focus on academic engagement. Student involvement in both curricular and extracurricular dimensions of higher education has, for a long time, been viewed as the key to academic success (Astin, 1993). Today, however, research is focusing more on engagement in the academic enterprise. This emphasis on engagement comes, in part, because of the recognition that a growing proportion of higher education students are adult, part-time, or commuter students who are not on campus enough to be involved in the extracurricular dimensions of academic life. In contrast to involvement, which is inherently up to the individual, engagement is being measured by examining the extent to which the institution is creating an environment that facilitates student learning and connection to the campus. In other words, the engagement research measures the relationship between student initiative and campus opportunities. This shift is in line with placing a greater emphasis on the institution's success or failure rather than focusing solely on the individual student. An increased emphasis on how campuses can be more engaging to their students is likely to be part of future discussions of campus climate in relationship to diversity (Kuh, 2001).

While some progress has been made with regard to diversifying the curriculum, there are still huge domains in the curriculum that are empty regarding race, class, and gender that need to be engaged. Nationally, we have talked more about diversifying the undergraduate curriculum than we have engaged in discussions about graduate education. It is imperative that these discussions occur with regard to graduate education, as graduate students, the scholars of tomorrow, will be the ones to fill the gaping holes in our knowledge regarding diverse groups. Unless we educate graduate students to look at diversity issues, efforts at the undergraduate level will remain patchwork and incomplete. Further, it is in graduate school that we train future leaders and validate what is seen as important and not important scholarship.

Institutional Viability

Much of the diversity efforts undertaken over the past decade have focused on improving the education and climate for students, it is becoming increasingly clear that diversity has a central role to play in the viability and vitality of our campuses. Diversity is a central issue that must be addressed. Within this dimension of diversity include discussions about mission, about staff and faculty diversity, issues of credibility, effectiveness, and attractiveness. This dimension examines the extent to which institutions are fully engaged in diversity rather than just engaging in diversity rhetoric.

Faculty and staff diversity, rather than simply being seen as important for students, must now be understood as central to the capacity of institutions to engage diversity at all levels, to interact with communities outside of the campus, to be credible and viable in working on diversity issues, and to have the expertise necessary in the realm of scholarship and education. Growing evidence, for example, now supports the idea that faculty diversity (especially in race/ethnicity and gender) is linked to curricular change; the inclusion of issues of race, class, gender, and sexual orientation in the educational process; and diversification of scholarship and pedagogical perspectives (Milem and Astin, 1993).

While the focus of the 1989 monograph was on student diversity, the present day situation suggests that it is even more important to discuss issues of faculty and staff diversity than ever before. Further, we know that 82 percent of all faculty are white, 5 percent are African American, 3 percent are Latino, 5 percent are Asian American, 0.4 percent are Native American, and 0.9 percent are non-resident aliens. White women and faculty of color are both severely underrepresented among full-time tenure track faculty, among faculty at the highest academic ranks, and in the most selective academic institutions. Until their representation within the faculty and administration changes, higher education will be slow to build the necessary capacity to be credible and to function in this very pluralistic society. Moreover, it is clear that the pipeline arguments are not sufficient to explain the lack of progress here. Just as with students, identifying talent is not easily done on campus when we use status quo methods (Moody, 2004; Smith and Associates, 1996; Tierney and Bensimon, 1996; Turner and Myers, 2000).

It seems clear that an additive approach to diversity will not work. Just having a diverse undergraduate student population or engaging in a series of diversity "activities" is not sufficient to bring about the kinds of changes necessary to truly produce institutional viability. There is a lot of work to be done. Institutions of higher education need to engage in serious assessment about diversity. This is difficult to do because institutions are worried and frightened about looking bad.

What messages emphasized in the original monograph are still important today? The 1989 monograph made several points about diversity that are still true and that are worth re-emphasizing today. These points include the following:

Language is important. It is important how groups are labeled and who is doing the labeling.

Disaggregation of data is also critically important. There are important within-group differences that get lost when data are lumped together. Analyzing data by "majority" and "minority" or even looking at groups such as Latinos and Asian Americans as homogenous will mask important differences within groups.

It is important to think of education as a K–16 system. The students who enter higher education come from the K–12 system that varies greatly depending on resource availability. Not all students have the same access to high quality academic preparation as others.

Institutions of higher education have not developed sufficient capacity to identify talented individuals and still rely too heavily on standardized testing. A new model for identifying which students will be successful in higher education is long overdue.

Institutions of higher education still look at students from diverse perspectives using a deficit model, focusing on background characteristics that predict failure rather than success. The focus needs to be on the institution and how it educates its students and creates a climate that allows all of its students to be successful.

Concerns about self-segregation are a white problem, not a problem for students of color. Research shows that identity-based efforts of students of color are linked to student success and satisfaction. There is, however, a negative relationship between white students engaging in white-only groups and learning outcomes.

Diversifying the faculty is still a key factor in achieving success for diverse students. Faculty members from diverse backgrounds have been shown to mentor students, bring new perspectives to the curriculum and to scholarship, and enhance the institution's ability to be successful in a variety of realms.

Assessment of diversity initiatives is crucial if we are to know what is working and what isn't and if we are to communicate the effect of diversity initiatives.

Leadership at all levels remains key to achieving diversity goals.

Following is the original Executive Summary written by Daryl Smith in 1989. The summary answers a series of questions covered in the monograph and is based on the state of the literature at that time. We thought it would be helpful to ask and re-answer these same questions to examine the extent to which things have changed and stayed the same. The new 2005 answers to the questions are in italics following the original answer.

Executive Summary

For years, researchers have forecast the increasing diversification of students in higher education as a result of changing demographics and a variety of other social and economic shifts. The diverse elements of today's student body include age, gender, ethnic and racial backgrounds, and increasing numbers of differently abled and part-time students. Despite the difficulties inherent in generalizing across such disparate groups and individuals, the issues higher education faces fundamentally relate to the capacity of institutions to function in a pluralistic environment. While it is unrealistic to assume that higher education will solve all these challenges independent of the rest of society, it is clear that the successful involvement of diverse populations has significant implications for education and for the nation.

What Is the Current Status of Enrollments, Graduation Rates, and the Campus Climate?

Although the makeup of today's student bodies is more diverse than 20 years ago, current enrollments suggest that this trend has reversed itself for some groups. Moreover, many students are clustered not only in segments of the postsecondary system but also in various levels and fields. Several recent national reports have sounded an alarm that the progress with respect to enrollments is not sufficient. Observers generally agree that retention overall and the retention rate for certain specific populations are critical problems for many institutions, even though surprisingly little is known about retention for most minority populations and for other nontraditional groups. One of the more troubling themes to emerge is that many campuses do not effectively involve students who are different. Students must confront stereotypic attitudes, unfamiliar values, ineffective teaching methods, and an organizational approach that may not support their efforts to succeed. While such concerns are prominent in the experience of minority students, issues of stereotyping, social isolation, and alienation are found in each of the literatures on women, disabled students, and adult learners as well. Indeed, in contemporary higher education, the condition of diversity is all too often a condition of alienation. Given these institutional patterns, the dominant focus on the preparation of students as the primary issue appears to be overemphasized. The questionable validity of many instruments used to predict performance and the evidence of other factors affecting performance suggest that other characteristics of students and noncognitive measures and more critically, the institutional role in student success, need to be considered.

As suggested in the new introduction to this monograph in the discussion of dimensions one and two of the diversity framework, we have made some progress in terms of providing access to higher education for historically underrepresented groups. Despite this progress, however, many groups of students of color still lag behind their white counterparts in terms of access to and graduation from higher education. They are underrepresented in four-year institutions and at the most selective institutions. Moreover, there are also far more individuals who identify themselves as multiracial, which has generated new research and may lead to new ways of thinking about majority and minority. However, because the overall demographics of many campuses has changed with respect to ethnicity and race, campuses can assume, as many do, that they are "done" with respect to diversity while ignoring issues of underrepresentation and significant achievement gaps.

Today as in the past, students from lower socioeconomic groups are the least likely to earn undergraduate degrees—a factor that has shown no improvement since the initial monograph was published. There is currently a stronger emphasis in current research on the role of social class in relationship to access and success in higher education. We now understand that it isn't only the inability to afford education that hinders low income students (although that continues to be a major concern), but that cultural and social capital plays a role in students' decisions about postsecondary education. There is also a lot more discussion and research available on the access and success of first-generation college students.

In terms of campus climate concerns, there is much more public discussion about gay, lesbian, bisexual, and transgendered students today, a topic left out of the original monograph. Also, more recent research on the "chilly climate" in higher education has not demonstrated the same kinds of findings as were discovered in the 1970s and 1980s. This has led researchers to think differently about how climate is measured.

Recent studies demonstrate that students who perceive that their institutions are committed to diversity are more likely to experience positive outcomes, including academic success, satisfaction with their education, and other positive outcomes. These findings show that there are positive effects associated with institutions that care about their climate for diversity. Despite these findings, research still demonstrates that the college environment is not perceived as welcoming and supportive for all student groups. Many students still experience isolation and a lack of support on their campuses. These concerns continue to warrant the attention of academic professionals.

What Theoretical Perspectives Might Be Useful?

The literatures on involvement, cultural pluralism, intergroup relations, and demography illuminate some of the issues present today on many campuses and provide a perspective that might be helpful in addressing them. Considerable theoretical and research evidence supports the importance of students' involvement and integration. Such evidence points to the need for increased opportunities for cooperative learning and significant interactions among peers and with faculty. The literature on intergroup relations suggests, however, that involvement cannot be achieved simply by putting people together. The quality of the environment, power relationships, degree of competition, levels of frustration, and institutional support all contribute to the quality of interaction and relationships. Furthermore, the literature on cultural pluralism suggests that the current notion of simply respecting differences is an oversimplification that avoids concerns about genuine differences in values and approaches and the ways in which institutional values also must change. The literature on demography indicates that as long as some groups are underrepresented, the experience of tokenism—including isolation and heightened visibility—will emerge. One of the greatest challenges of diversity rests on integrating the objectives of involvement into the fabric of pluralism.

The theoretical frameworks suggested here are still useful today. In addition, there are some new frameworks that have been developed since the book was published that shed light on important diversity issues. These include a focus on engagement in lieu of a focus on involvement; more emphasis on the importance of social and cultural capital and how social class influences access to higher education; recent work on critical theory and critical race theory that has focused on power and structural inequities and how these influence how higher education responds to diversity; the intersections and complexities of identity; whiteness studies; and notions of multicontextuality (Ali, 2003; Darder, 1991; Doane and Bonilla-Silva, 2003; Frable, 1997; Guinier and Torres, 2002; hooks, 1994; Ibarra, 2000; McDonough, 1997; Solorzano, 1998).

What Are the Patterns in Institutions Labeled Successful?

Five major themes emerge from a variety of studies looking at successful institutions. These institutions:

1. Focus on students' success and provide the tools for success;
2. Have begun to develop programs for increased coordination with elementary and secondary grades and for enhanced articulation between community colleges and four-year colleges and universities;
3. Dedicate energy and resources to creating an accepting environment that nourishes and encourages success;
4. Have access to good information that focuses on the institution and students;
5. Include leaders in the faculty and administration who provide strong direction for these efforts.

In addition to the insights that can be developed from successful institutions, lessons can be learned from women's colleges and from historically black institutions. Despite notable challenges to their survival, these institutions have contributed significantly to the success of women and to African American students, particularly in that they provide an environment that believes in the potential and success of their students and involves them in all aspects of the institution. Central to their success is the presence of many African American and female faculty and administrators.

Today, special purpose institutions still have something to teach the rest of higher education (Allen, 1992; Boyer, 1997; Carnegie Foundation, 1989; Tidball, Smith, Tidball, and Wolf-Wendel, 1999). These institutions model the ideals of having high expectations of students, providing the support necessary for students to succeed, providing role models, a mission that intentionally focuses on student success, and, a culture deeply embedded with a focus on student success and serving the community. Research shows that these factors continue to be necessary to achieve student success. Further, special focus colleges offer a model for institutions that focuses on institutional commitment rather than on student deficits. Research shows that good education matters and that when students are exposed to a good education background factors seem to matter less.

What Are the Fundamental Issues of Organizing for Diversity?

The basic conceptual framework for many of the more traditional responses to diversity has focused essentially on *student assistance*. These approaches address the particular needs or "problems" felt to be barriers to students' success. Many institutions have broadened these efforts to include *institutional accommodations,* which acknowledges that some of the barriers to success rest with the institution itself. While these accommodations are steps in the right direction, they are not sufficient in themselves. They should be viewed as part of a broader effort included in the capacity of institutions to *organize for diversity*. At the core of this effort will be an organization's ability to educate in a pluralistic society for a pluralistic world. To reach such a place requires a shift not only in thinking but also in framing the questions we ask. The challenges of such fundamental transformation mean grappling with a number of complex issues:

Diversity of faculty and staff. Diverse perspectives are required to develop organizations sensitive to pluralism. Despite overwhelming agreement that diversity in faculty and staff is essential for all institutions, the goal may prove difficult. The lack of growth in enrollments and the absence of students from nontraditional groups in the educational pipeline—particularly at the graduate and professional levels—threaten institutional goals for hiring women and minorities. Barriers to this effort are not only in a perceived lack of available candidates: A serious question exists as to whether institutions are promoting and retaining faculty members from nontraditional groups already present. Efforts to retain and promote from within are as important as increasing the pool of applicants.

Mission and values. The issue of values emerges at a number of levels. Perhaps the most challenging has to do with the ways in which students perceive that the values and perspectives they bring are not appreciated and may even put them in conflict with the institution's norms and behaviors. Cooperation/conflict and individualism/community are two value domains where preferred modes of relating and learning may conflict with dominant institutional values. Institutions need to reflect on some of these values and on whether the institution is promoting assimilation rather than pluralism. Institutions must be very clear in differentiating between those values and goals that facilitate learning and the mission of the institution itself, and those values that leave individuals and groups relegated to the margin.

Educating for diversity. Ignorance and insensitivity are commonly present on campuses, but institutions are beginning to articulate a commitment to educate all students and other members of the community for living in a pluralistic world. The content of the curriculum, styles of teaching, and modes of assessment are three elements in this effort.

Dealing with conflict. The conditions for conflict are present on many campuses. Indeed, conflict may be an essential part of the process institutions will experience to clarify the many complex issues involved in creating pluralistic communities. Conflict may be part of the institutional learning process.

The quality of interaction. A growing body of research evidence reflects the importance of students' involvement with the institution and peers and between students and faculty. While we know much less about the nature of this dynamic for many nontraditional groups, the quality of interaction, the attitudes of faculty, staff, and students toward one another, and the perception of the climate on campus must be evaluated and addressed.

The perceived conflict between quality and diversity. The continuing message that a fundamental conflict exists between diversity and quality is perhaps the most compelling argument for reshaping the questions and the discourse about this topic. We *can* broaden our understanding about quality without diluting expectations for learning or for the curriculum, but to do so will require reframing our understanding about the meaning of quality, the definition of standards, performance criteria, and assessment. Many current approaches to assessment of students, programs, or faculty tend to devalue the performance of those who are different. Particular attention must be paid to the role of standardized testing and the increasing alarm about its validity for many nontraditional populations.

The list of fundamental issues necessary for organizing for diversity stated above remain unchanged today. Framing issues properly, as noted earlier, continues as an important concern today. We still need to make progress in diversifying the faculty and staff, we need to think about the centrality of diversity to the institution's mission and values, we need to augment the curriculum to educate for diversity, we need to deal with conflict, and we need to address the perceived conflict between quality and diversity. There are many other elements that are emerging as central to success on diversity and good research, as described here, that continue to develop in this area (for example, Smith and Associates, 2000). Two other elements that we would add are the diversity framework developed by Daryl Smith subsequent to her 1989 monograph and an increased emphasis on the need for assessment.

The diversity dimensions framework discussed in the introduction has really matured and been refined since the original monograph was published in 1989. The four dimensions of diversity—access and success, campus climate and intergroup relations, education and scholarship, and institutional viability and vitality—are a helpful way of thinking about and organizing campus diversity initiatives. The diversity dimensions are separate, but interrelated. The dimensions offer a lens through which campus activities or initiatives can be focused to enhance the vitality and viability of institutions (Smith, 1995; Smith and Associates, 1997).

The need to assess campus progress in response to diversity has grown in importance over the last several decades. Assessment is important because it can provide a framework for evaluating the effectiveness of work on diversity at the institutional level over a sustained period of time. Using organizational learning and a framework like the dimensions of diversity, institutions can agree on indicators that will mark progress, collect manageable data that will provide guidance on what is working and what is not working, and provide locations where meaningful discussions about progress on diversity can occur. Assessment can also help to identify factors that provide momentum for diversity work and can be a vehicle through which institutions communicate the benefits of diversity initiatives to various audiences—legislators, trustees, faculty, students, administrators, and the public. As institutions of higher education have become more accountable for the way they are using resources, the need to assess diversity initiatives also becomes more important. While assessment is discussed in the initial monograph, it wasn't emphasized as much as it might have been if the monograph had been written today (Bensimon and Associates, 2004; Smith, 1999; Musil and Associates, 1999; Nettles and Associates, 2002).

What Are the Implications of the Challenge of Diversity?

The challenge of diversity is national in scope. Given the complexities involved, no recipes are available to create truly pluralistic organizations. Institutions and policy makers can take some steps, however, to facilitate the process of adequately responding to diversity.

1. A comprehensive institutional assessment can provide important data from which priorities can be identified.

Cross-institutional research can identify successful institutions, identify ways in which involvement can be promoted, and clarify often conflicting material in the literature.

Coordination among the educational sectors can improve articulation and movement between levels and types of institutions.

Developing programs and funds can increase the number of students who enter teaching at all levels.

2. Organizations that succeed in meeting this challenge can also play a significant role in educating all future teachers and citizens to function in a diverse culture.

Providing increased local, state, and national financial aid will make access more possible for virtually every population of students.

Sustained commitment and effort rather than episodic interest will be required.

Leadership plays a central role, not only in setting goals and providing resources but also in framing the questions and setting the tone for deliberations.

If a single lesson is to be learned from the literature on diversity, it is that we cannot simply "add and stir." The challenges are many, but it is clear that the process of meeting them will bring great benefits to all members of the community and to the institution itself. The resources of diversity within an organization are more likely to prepare it for the future than any other resource.

As in the initial monograph, the challenge of diversity remains much the same as it did in 1989. The factors cited as concerns above still need to be accomplished today. Today, however, we would replace the term "challenge" with the term "imperative." Indeed, because of the relative lack of progress made on these issues since 1989, it feels more urgent today that we address these concerns. This monograph argues that diversity goes to the heart of whether our institutions and our society will be viable. Our viability rests on our capacity to fully engage diversity at all levels and to successfully educate all students for a very pluralistic society and world.

One way to accomplish this is to think about diversity in the same ways that we now think of technology—as a fundamental, central component of how we do things. The parallel between technology and diversity is an important one. Higher education has adapted to the increasingly technologically oriented way of doing things by providing access to technology at all levels of the institution, building infrastructures to support technology, educating students about technology, and infusing it into the institution. Higher education has allowed technology to change what students learn, how they learn it, what scholarship looks like, and how we operate on a daily basis. In the same way, we need to ask institutions to respond to diversity. Can we come to see diversity in the same way that we see technology? Can we really alter our institutions in the same kind of ways to support diversity that we are doing to support technology? If we can't do this on our campuses, how do we expect our cities, our neighborhoods, or our country to do it?

References

Ali, S. (2003). *Mixed-race, post-race: Gender, new ethnicities and cultural practices.* New York: Berg.

Allen, W. (1992). The color of success. *Harvard Educational Review, 62*(1), 26–44.

Antonio, A. L. (2001). Diversity and the influence of friendship groups in college. *Review of Higher Education, 25*(1), 63–89.

Astin, A. W. (1993). *What matters in college? Four critical years revisited.* San Francisco: Jossey-Bass.

Barkan, E. (2000). *The guilt of nations.* New York: Norton.

Beckham, E. F. (Ed.). (2000). *Diversity, democracy, and higher education: A view from three nations.* Washington, DC: Association of American Colleges and Universities.

Bensimon, E. M., Polkington, D. E., Bauman, G., and Vallejo, E. (2004). Doing research that makes a difference. *Journal of Higher Education, 75*(1).

Bikson, T. A. (1996). Educating a globally prepared workforce: New research on college and corporate perspectives. *Liberal Education, 82*(2), 12–19.

Borrego, S. (2003). *Class matters: Beyond access to inclusion.* Washington, DC: NASPA.

Bowen, W. G., and Bok, D. (1998). *The shape of the river: Long-term consequences of considering race in college and university admissions.* Princeton, NJ: Princeton University Press.

Boyer, P. (1997). *Native American colleges: Progress and prospects.* Princeton, NJ: Carnegie Foundation for the Advancement of Teaching.

Brewer, M. B. (2000). Reducing prejudice through cross categorization: Effects of multiple social identities. In S. Oskamp (Ed.), *Reducing prejudice and discrimination* (pp. 165–184). Mahwah, NJ: Erlbaum.

Carnegie Foundation for the Advancement of Teaching. (1989). *Tribal colleges: Shaping the future of Native America. A special report.* Lawrenceville, NJ: Princeton University Press.

Carnevale, A. P. (1999). Diversity in higher education: Why corporate America cares. *Diversity Digest, 3*(3). Available at: http://www.diversityweb.org/Digest/Sp99/corporate.html.

Chang, M., Astin, A., and Kim, D. (2004). Cross-racial interaction among undergraduates: Some consequences, causes, and patterns. *Research in Higher Education 45*(5), 529–553.

Chang, M., Witt, D., Jones, J., and Hakuta, K. (Eds.). (1999). *Compelling interest: Examining the evidence on racial dynamics in higher education. A report of the AERA Panel on Racial Dynamics in Colleges and Universities.* Palo Alto, CA: Center for Comparative Studies in Race and Ethnicity, Stanford University.

Chang, M. J. (1999). Does racial diversity matter? The educational impact of a racially diverse undergraduate population. *Journal of College Student Development, 40,* 377–395.

Cloete, N., Muller, J., Makgoba, M. W., and Ekong, D. (Eds.). (1997). *Knowledge, identity, and curriculum transformation in South Africa.* Capetown, South Africa: Masker Miller Longman.

Cox, T. H., Jr. (1993). Cultural diversity in organizations: Theory, research, and practice. San Francisco: Berrett-Koehler.

Cross, M., Cloete, N., Beckham, E. F., Harper, A., Inidresan, J., and Musil, C. (Eds.). (1999). *Diversity and unity: The role of higher education in building democracy.* Capetown, South Africa: Maskew Miller Longman.

Darder, A. (1991). *Culture and power in the classroom: A critical foundation for bicultural education.* New York: Bergin and Garvey.

Doane, A. W., and Bonilla-Silva, E. (Eds.). (2003). *White out: The continuing significance of race.* New York: Routledge.

Espiritu, Y. L. (1997). *Asian American women and men.* Thousand Oaks, CA: Sage.

Ford Foundation. (1998). National Survey of Voters. unpublished manuscript.

Frable, D.E.S. (1997). Gender, racial, ethnic, sexual, and class identities. *Annual Review of Psychology, 48,* 139–162.

Gandara, P. (1999). *Priming the pump: Strategies for increasing the achievement of underrepresented minority undergraduates.* New York: College Board.

Guarasci, R., Cornewell, G. H., and Associates. (1997). *Democratic education in an age of difference.* San Francisco: Jossey-Bass.

Gudeman, R. H. (2000). College missions, faculty teaching, and student outcomes in a context of low diversity. In *Does diversity make a difference? Three research studies on diversity in college classrooms* (pp. 37–60). Washington, DC: ACE and AAUP. Available at: http://www.acenet.edu/programs/caree/diversity.cfm.

Guinier, L., and Torres, G. (2002). *The miner's canary: Enlisting race, resisting power, transforming democracy.* Cambridge, MA: Harvard.

Gurin, P., Dey, E. L., Hurtado, S., and Gurin, G. (2002). Diversity and higher education: Theory and impact on educational outcomes. *Harvard Educational Review, 72*(3), 330–366.

Heller, D. (Ed.). (2002). *Condition of access: Higher education for lower income students.* Washington, DC: ACE/Praeger.

Herek, G. M., and Capitanio, J. P. (1996). "Some of my best friends": Intergroup contact, concealable stigma, and heterosexuals' attitudes toward gay men and lesbians. *Personality and Social Psychology Bulletin, 22,* 412–424.

hooks, bell. (1994). *Teaching to transgress.* New York: Routledge.

Hune, S., and Chan, K. S. (1997). Special focus: Asian Pacific American demographic and educational trends. In D. J. Carter and R. Wilson (Eds.), Fifteenth annual status report on minorities in higher education (pp. 39–67). Washington, DC: American Council on Education.

Hurtado, S. (1994). The institutional climate for talented Latino students. *Research in Higher Education, 35,* 21–41.

Hurtado, S. (1996). How diversity affects teaching and learning: A climate of inclusion has a positive effect on learning outcomes. *Educational Record, 66,* 27–29.

Hurtado, S., Engberg, M. E., Ponjuan, L., Landreman, L. (2002). Students' precollege preparation for participation in a diverse democracy. *Research in Higher Education, 43*(2), 163–186.

Hurtado, S., Milem, J. F., Clayton-Pedersen, A. R., and Allen, W. R. (1998). Enhancing campus climates for racial/ethnic diversity: Educational policy and practice. *Review of Higher Education, 21,* 279–302.

Ibarra, R. A. (2000). *Beyond affirmative action: Reframing the context of higher education.* Madison, WI: University of Wisconsin Press.

Kuh, G. D. (2001). Assessing what matters to student learning: Inside the National Survey of Student Engagement. *Change, 33*(3), 10–17, 66.

Loden, M., and Rosener, J. B. (1991). *Workforce America: Managing employee diversity as a vital resource.* Homewood, IL: Business One Irwin.

Lowe, E. Y., Jr. (Ed.). (1999). *Promise and dilemma: Perspectives on racial diversity and higher education* (pp. 135–142). Princeton, NJ: Princeton University Press.

Marin, P. (2000). The educational possibility of multi-racial/multi-ethnic college classrooms. In *Does diversity make a difference: Three research studies on diversity in college classrooms* (pp. 61–83). Washington, DC: ACE and AAUP.

Maruyama, G., and Moreno, J. F. (2000). University faculty views about the value of diversity on campus and in the classroom. In *Does diversity make a difference: Three research studies on diversity in college classrooms* (pp. 9–35). Washington, DC: ACE and AAUP.

Maton, K. I., and Hrabowski, F. A. (2004). Increasing the number of African American Ph.D.'s in the sciences and engineering. *American Psychologist, 59*(6), 547–556.

McDonough, P. (1997). Choosing colleges: How social class and schools structure opportunity. Albany, NY: SUNY Press.

Milem, J. F., and Astin, H. S. (1993). The changing composition of the faculty: What does it really mean for diversity? *Change, 25*(2), 21–27.

Moody, J. (2004). *Faculty diversity.* New York: Routledge/Falmer.

Morrison, A. M. (1992). *The new leaders: Guidelines on leadership diversity in America.* San Francisco: Jossey-Bass.

Mortenson, T. G. (2003a, June). College continuation rates for recent high school graduates, 1959 to 2002. *Postsecondary Education Opportunity,* no. 132.

Mortenson, T. G. (2003b, November). Undergraduate degree completion by age 25 to 29 for those who enter college 1947 to 2002. *Postsecondary Education Opportunity,* no. 137.

Mortenson, T. G. (2004, May). Family income and higher education opportunity, 1970 to 2002. *Postsecondary Education Opportunity,* no. 143.

Moses, Y. (1999). *Quality, excellence, and diversity.* In D. G. Smith, L. E. Wolf, and T. Levitan (Eds.), Studying diversity in higher education. *New Directions in Higher Education,* No. 81. (pp. 9–20). San Francisco: Jossey-Bass.

Musil, C. M., Garcia, M., Hudguns, C. A., Nettles, M. T., Sedlacek, W. E., and Smith, D. G. (1999). *To form a more perfect union: Campus diversity initiatives.* Washington, DC: Association of American Colleges and Universities.

Nakanishi, D. T., and Nishida, T. Y. (Eds.). (1995). *The Asian American educational experience.* New York: Routledge.

National Cener for Public Policy and Higher Education. (2003). Losing ground: A national report on the affordability of American higher education. Available at http://www.high-ereducation.org/reports/losing_ground/ar.shtml.

Nettles, M., Sedlacek, W., Smith, D., Musil, C., Hudgins, C., and Garcia, M. (2002). *Assessing diversity on college and university campuses.* Washington, DC: Association of American Colleges and Universities.

Orfield, G. (Ed.). (2001). *Diversity challenged: Evidence on the impact of affirmative action.* Cambridge, MA: Harvard Educational Review.

Padilla, F. M. (1997). *The struggle of Latino/Latina university students: In search of a liberating education.* New York: Routledge.

Pettigrew, T. F., and Tropp, L. R. (2000). Does intergroup contact reduce prejudices? Recent meta-analytic findings. In S. Oskamp (Ed.), *Reducing prejudice and discrimination* (pp. 93–114). Mahwah, NJ: Erlbaum.

Rendon, L. I., and Hope, R. O. (Eds.). (1996). *Educating a new majority: Transforming America's educational system for diversity.* San Francisco: Jossey-Bass.

Schoem, D., Frankel, L., Zúñiga, X., and Lewis, E. A. (Eds.). (1993). *Multicultural teaching in the university* (pp. 249–259). Westport, CT: Praeger.

Sedlacek, W. (2004). *Beyond the big test: Noncognitive assessment in higher education.* San Francisco: Jossey-Bass.

Smith, D. G. (1995). Organizational implications of diversity. In M. Chemers, S. Oskamp, and M. Costanza (Eds.), *Diversity in organizations.* Newbury Park, CA: Sage.

Smith, D. G. (1999). Strategic evaluation: An imperative for the future of campus diversity. In M. Cross, N. Cloete, E. F. Beckham, A. Harper, J. Indiresan, and C. Musil (Eds.), *Diversity and unity: The role of higher education in building democracy.* Capetown, South Africa: Maskew Miller Longman.

Smith, D. G., and Associates. (1997). *Diversity works: The emerging picture of how students benefit.* Washington, DC: Association of American Colleges and Universities.

Smith, D. G., Garcia, M., Hudgins, C., Nettles, M., Sedlacek, W. (2000). *A diversity research agenda: What more do we need to know?* Washington, DC: Association of American Colleges and Universities.

Smith, D. G., Wolf, L. E., Busenberg, B., and Associates. (1996). *Achieving faculty diversity: Debunking the myths.* Washington, DC: Association of American Colleges and Universities.

Solorzano, D. G. (1998). Critical race theory, race and gender microaggressions, and the experience of Chicana and Chicano scholars. *International Journal of Qualitative Studies in Education, 11*(1), 121–136.

Steele, C. (1999). A threat in the air: How stereotypes shape intellectual identity and performance. In E. Y. Lowe, Jr. (Ed.), *Promise and dilemma*. Princeton, NJ: Princeton University Press.

Tatum, B. D. (1997). *"Why are all the Black kids sitting together in the cafeteria?" And other conversations about race.* New York: Basic Books.

Tidball, M. E., Smith, D. G., Tidball, C. S., and Wolf-Wendel, L. E. (1999). *Taking women seriously: Lessons and legacies for educating the majority.* Phoenix, AZ: American Council on Education and Oryx Press.

Tierney, W. G. (1993). *Building communities of difference: Higher education in the twenty-first century.* Westport, CT: Bergin and Garvey.

Tierney, W. G., and Bensimon, E. M. (1996). *Promotion and tenure: Community and socialization in academe.* Albany, NY: SUNY Press.

Treisman, U. (1992). Studying students studying calculus: A look at the lives of minority mathematics students in college. *College Mathematics Journal, 23*, 362–372.

Turner, C.S.V., and Myers, S. L. (2000). Faculty of color in academe: Bittersweet success. Needham Heights, MA: Allyn and Bacon.

WICHE. (2004). *Knocking at the college door: Projections of high school graduates by state, income, and race/ethnicity, 1988–2018.* Boulder, CO: WICHE.

Zandy, J. (Ed.) (2001). *What we hold in common: An introduction to working class studies.* New York: Feminist Press.

Acknowledgments

I am grateful to many people who were helpful and supportive in the development of this monograph. Numbers of students and colleagues took the time to evaluate the manuscript and to assist me in the development of the ideas for this topic. Fay Rulau and Jane Gray were patient and diligent in the preparations of the document, and without the support and editorial suggestions of Barbara Bergmann, it would read with much less clarity. The anonymous reviewers were invaluable in their suggestions, and the staff at the ERIC Clearinghouse on Higher Education were always there to provide whatever guidance and support I needed.

I especially wish to acknowledge the work of many scholars whose material has not been published by mainstream presses and journals but whose work provided support and insight into the many complex challenges involved in addressing the topic of diversity. Their relative invisibility is symbolic of the problems inherent in this topic. Their work is very important.

Finally, I wish to salute the many administrators, faculty members, and students who are currently engaged in trying to meet the challenges of diversity through the transformation of their institutions. I hope that this report supports their efforts and provides an impetus for further action.

Original Introduction

FOR YEARS, RESEARCHERS have forecast the increasing diversification of students in higher education as a result of changing demographics and a variety of other societal and economic shifts (Frances, 1980; Hodgkinson, 1985). Indeed, dramatic changes have taken place in the composition of student bodies in American higher education. The diverse elements of today's student body include age, ethnic background, sexual preference, and ever-increasing numbers of "differently" abled, part-time, international, and commuting students. Despite the difficulties inherent in generalizing across such disparate groups and individuals, this report suggests that the issue higher education is facing fundamentally relate to the capacity of institutions to function in a pluralistic environment. In this context, the report addresses the changes in demographics that have taken place and raises some of the critical issues that emerge in responding to the challenge of diversity.

Historically, as institutions have evaluated their success with different groups of students, most of the questions have focused on success in terms of the student and attributed success or failure to the student's background characteristics. Out of that research came a wealth of information on students' background characteristics, personality factors, and family origins and the relationship between those characteristics and academic success. While a rationale exists for this approach, the result has been that the problems and the responsibility to be successful were defined in terms of the individual. An extensive literature now suggests, however, that the issues facing nontraditional students go beyond their individual or group backgrounds—and even beyond the particular interaction of their background with the institutional environment—directly to the question of whether institutions are designed to deal with diversity. The theme of alienation pervades the literature. It is a powerful voice in the literature concerning racial and ethnic minorities. It is also present in the literature focusing on women, the disabled, and other nontraditional groups. A synthesis of this literature suggests that our research, programs, and institutional and public policy must be focused not only on the "needs" of each nontraditional group but also on the organizational issues institutions must address (Boyd, 1982; Burrell, 1980; Jaramillo, 1988; Lunneborg and Lunneborg, 1985; Pearson, Shavlik, and Touchton, 1989; Verdugo, 1986; Wilkerson, 1987; Zambrana, 1987).

In light of the broad literature describing the experiences of many of these student groups, one of the central questions that emerges is how higher education will meet the challenge of diversity. Not enough progress has been made; indeed, in a number of areas it has been reversed. Although an alarm has been sounded, the calls to action may not yet adequately address the complexity and depth of the issues involved. By looking at many of the groups that have been at the margin of institutions of higher education, this monograph attempts to examine some of the critical issues that develop when an institution addresses the challenge of diversity.

It must be noted at the outset that the challenge of diversity is not new to this decade, to higher education, or to this country (Anderson, 1987; Peterson and Associates, 1978). Indeed, since its founding, the United States has been viewed as a major social experiment precisely because of its efforts to create a single society involving people of diverse ethnic, religious, and national backgrounds. Traditionally, the metaphor for such an effort has been the "melting pot" in which people come from all over and create a new American culture. That image has increasingly been called into question. At its most basic, today's challenge calls for the creation of a society in which individual differences are respected and allowed to coexist. While such a statement is easy to make and to support, the form of that society is not very clear while the challenges of creating it are very real. The process of creating communities requires decisions and interactions that address fundamental values, preferences, or rights, some of which may conflict. Such decisions are also affected by levels of communication, styles of interaction, or perceptions about others that are related to a person's background. They are, in other words, strongly affected by diversity. Thus, the consequences of heterogeneity have dramatic implications at all levels of society and at all levels of the organizations within that society.

Clearly, we have not yet achieved a vision of what a pluralistic community should look like. Indeed, it is not clear that we even agree on all the elements of that vision. Volumes have been written addressing these questions: *The Negro in the United States* (Frazier, 1957), *An American Dilemma* (Myrdal, 1962), *The Nature of Prejudice* (Allport, 1954), and "New Black-White Patterns" (Pettigrew, 1985) are examples of such scholarship. It is therefore unrealistic to assume that higher education can on its own achieve pluralistic communities that do not reflect the problems in the larger society or that higher education can, independent of other institutions, solve all the challenges of diversity. But just as the issues of a culturally pluralistic society must be high on the national agenda, so too must they be high on the agendas of colleges and universities across the country. Not only will the successful involvement of diverse populations tip the balance between institutional survival and failure and between educational quality and mediocrity, but, more significantly, the social implications will spread far beyond the academy.

Numerous national reports concerned in particular about the participation of minorities in higher education have articulated eloquent appeals for national and educational attention to this issue. One of the most recent, *One-Third of a Nation* (Commission on Minority Participation, 1988), is a joint undertaking of the American Council on Education and the Education Commission of the States. It sounds a warning:

> *America is moving backward—not forward—in its efforts to achieve the full participation of minority citizens in the life and prosperity of the nation. . . . If we allow these disparities to continue, the United States will inevitably suffer a compromised quality of life and a lower standard of living (p. 1).*

Most scholars tend to mark the late 1960s as the beginning of the changes in diversity in higher education. It is important to recognize, however, that colleges and universities have been adjusting to and accommodating "new" kinds of students almost since their founding. Although their efforts are most notable for their lack of success, attempts to educate Native Americans were part of the founding principles of a number of colonial colleges (laCounta, 1987). The move toward coeducation in the late 19th and early 20th centuries and the introduction of older students with the passage of the GI Bill following World War II provide examples of a broadening diversity in the populations that entered the academy before the Sixties (Lasser, 1987; Wilson, 1987b). While ways in which students and institutions accommodated the new arrivals can be cited in each case, the need for changes that never occurred is more evident.

Earlier efforts to achieve diversity notwithstanding, the past two decades have witnessed a dramatic shift in the demographic makeup of society as a whole as well as an influx of new students in higher education that are more diverse than ever before. As such, the past 20 years have presented a challenge to American higher education that is deeper and more significant than any changes that preceded them.

Caveats

This monograph focuses on the challenges of diversity facing colleges and universities today. To attempt such a task, however, first requires a recognition of some of the limitations inherent in the process, including the ability to generalize and the limits of language.

The risk always exists that in attempting to address the broader issues of diversity, as this monograph does, the perspective of particular groups will become so generalized as to be unrecognizable. The reality is that important differences exist in the issues, histories, and experiences of specific groups of students—women, racial and ethnic minorities, the disabled. Certainly, the issues of child care faced by a student who is also a single parent are experienced differently from a student dealing with racial discrimination (Pounds, 1987). It will be suggested, however, that unless institutions come to grips with diversity and the issues related to it, it will be difficult to address specific issues brought by individual groups.

Researchers must always be prepared to struggle with the challenges presented by the need to summarize, to generalize, and to reach conclusions, while at the same time recognizing the distinctive experiences of particular groups. It is ironic that in stressing this distinctiveness, we are concurrently creating classifications that are quickly rendered inadequate. We classify people into groups by gender, age, minority, disability. We classify institutions as two-year colleges, research universities, private or public institutions. It quickly becomes apparent that these groupings are themselves too simplistic (Hughes, 1983; Pounds, 1987).

Too often the definition of "handicap" conjures up the image of a wheelchair. The institutional response to the differently abled then is to build ramps, a modification of no consequence to someone who is deaf or learning disabled. Those with learning disabilities are an important part of this group yet have very different needs based not only on the handicap itself but also on the fact that this handicap is not visible (Schmidt and Sprandel, 1982). The literature frequently describes the Latino population without recognizing that this group includes people from very diverse backgrounds whose experiences in colleges and universities are not at all uniform (Burgos-Sasscer, 1987). The census classifies as "Hispanic" those of Mexican American, Puerto Rican, Cuban, and Central or South American origin (Brown, Rosen, and Hill, 1980). Of the 17.3 million people classified as Hispanic in 1985, over 10 million were Mexican Americans and 2.6 million Puerto Ricans (McKenna and Ortiz, 1988; Salganik and Maw, 1987). Four hundred eighty-one tribes are classified as Native American, each with its own traditions yet each one sharing some part of the experience of being grouped together as one.

The Asian American population is another important example of this issue. The classification "Asian American" includes, among others, the experiences of those of Japanese, Chinese, Vietnamese, Cambodian, Korean, Philippine, and Pacific Island origins. While over 60 Asian American subgroups are described in the literature (Carter, Pearson, and Shavlik, 1988), much of the literature either categorizes all of these peoples together or discusses the experiences of just one or two of them, ignoring the rest. Sensitivity is expressed in the literature by those concerned about Asian Americans. Asians are assumed to be an example of the "model" minority group that has made a successful transition to higher education, with their only issues being related to the burdens of overachievement and overenrollment. These assumptions ignore the wide variations among their subgroups and ignore the issues of racial discrimination, access, and success that do exist (Hsia, 1987, 1988; Sue, 1977, 1979).

By the same token, almost all the literature dealing with African American populations, women, adults, and the disabled increasingly points to the need to acknowledge the very great differences in individuals and subgroups that exist. Gender, for example, provides an important division for every other subgroup. Women of color face invisibility when certain issues facing those in this group are ignored under discussions of race or gender.

Thus, the danger of overgeneralizing on the one hand and being so specific on the other makes it difficult to come to any conclusions. This danger is one that institutions and scholars of higher education must confront, as it represents one of the difficult challenges of diversity itself. Nevertheless, it is through the various literatures on specific groups that this monograph was developed. Clearly, it would be impossible to adequately review the separate literatures that now exist on the adult learner, the African American student, the Latino student, the disabled student, and so on. It is not the intent of this monograph to do that. These literatures, however, are critical to the topic— and they have been reviewed to try to bring together the common themes that address diversity.

Another caveat involves the problem of language—a problem that takes two forms. The first is the question of how to describe the various groups being discussed in a way that respects their traditions and preferences. Our language is in constant flux, and it takes time for consensus to develop about the naming of groups. The once common use of such terms as "minority" and "black" has now shifted. In the meantime, choices have been made that attempt to respect current preferences. For example, this monograph uses the term "Latino" as the term of choice, despite the fact that the Census Bureau uses the term "Hispanic" for data collection. Despite the Census Bureau's classification of American Indians as Native Americans, this monograph uses the former as the identification to be used, except when referring to population tables. References to physical and learning disabilities or impairments can be controversial. As those who are "differently abled" achieve a greater degree of visibility and power within society, efforts will no doubt continue to find a "label" that feels suitable (Duffy, 1989). This monograph refers to those who are differently abled as the disabled because of the literature in this area. The issue of labels is important and significant and thus controversial.

Another nomenclature issue is reflected in the extreme sensitivity that certain words have to various readers. Racism—or institutional racism—is increasingly being "named" on campuses as one fundamental cause of the problems facing campuses today. Others resist using such terms because of the defensiveness they cause. Nevertheless, common use of the phrase "qualified women or minorities," for example, reveals many troubling assumptions. We do not usually say "qualified whites." One cannot ignore the role of racism, sexism, and homophobia as they affect institutional practice and students' experiences. The emphasis in this monograph is on illuminating some of the emerging issues that campuses need to address.

The literature on the topic of diversity is very uneven, both in its quality and in the topics under discussion. The vast majority of the early literature on diversity, for example, focused on African American students (Myrdal, 1962; Pettigrew, 1985; White and Sedlacek, 1987). Very little has been written to date on Cambodian, Vietnamese, or Korean students, although some important studies on different Asian groups are included in the literature on counseling and human services (Sue, 1979, 1981). Surprisingly little research on Chicanos has been undertaken until recently (Webster, 1984). What is written on the disabled tends to focus on program development, with much less available on the students themselves, their satisfaction and retention, or other issues (Jarrow, 1987).

A final caveat: Such a complex topic as diversity inevitably raises questions and problems that few societies—let alone institutions—have solved to all groups' satisfaction. The process of evaluating success in particular creates its own challenges. To a disenfranchised person, *some* progress is not very comforting, while to an administrator trying to create change, some progress might be all that can be expected. This monograph attempts to look at the question of success with both these perspectives in mind.

Framing the Question

The last section addressed the importance of nomenclature, for "how the problem is named involves alternative scenarios, each with its own facts, values, judgments, and emotions" (Edelman, 1977, p. 29). This concept is not simply an abstract one: It is a central part of the thesis of this monograph and one of the most difficult challenges facing decision makers. For example, when retention is named as the student dropout rate, we imply a problem with the student (Jaramillo, 1988). When we define retention as an institution's graduation rate, we focus on the institution. Furthermore, "as long as we condone the use of metaphors [that] conjure up a scenario of individual initiative and responsibility for educational failure, change will not occur" (Jaramillo, 1988, p. 27). This issue is most important, because the definition of a problem can dramatically affect the solutions sought, which has particular implications for the education of minorities, where too often failure has been focused on the student and the student's background. But the issue can be found in the approach of institutions to virtually all groups on the margin. It is also reflected in the development of new curricular approaches where early efforts focused on the absence of women or minorities from the curriculum. As curricula have been transformed, entire new fields and questions have emerged that point out the deficits in the canon rather than the deficits in women and minorities (McIntosh, 1989).

Despite theoretical models in higher education stressing that the outcomes of education are the result of complex interactions between the student and the institution, much of the literature, programs, and research have focused on the student and the characteristics of the student that lead to success. Framing the questions in this way deemphasizes organizational issues and organizational change (Willie and Edmonds, 1978). Carefully framing the question is an essential element in meeting the challenge of diversity.

The Status of Diversity

IT IS EASIER to talk about a desire to create a report card for higher education—to evaluate its success—than to actually do it. While some objective data are available, success also depends upon the choice of relevant criteria. This choice and the interpretation of the data vary depending upon the view one brings to the study. Moreover, it is difficult to imagine discussing higher education without reflecting the multidimensionality of the system. Great variation is present within the system on most any criterion. In evaluating the response to diversity, however, the three most common measures involve patterns of enrollment, retention through completion of degree programs, and the institutional climate. The following sections evaluate higher education as a system in these terms.

Enrollment

How successful has higher education been in achieving a system of open access to diverse populations? The answer to this question depends in part on the specific criteria of success one wishes to employ. Once again, framing the question becomes critical. One can compare factors to the distant past, to the recent past, to population demographics, and to an ideal of what "ought to be." A number of studies outline areas of progress, areas of decline, and areas of stagnation (Commission on Minority Participation, 1988; Green, 1989; Pettigrew, 1985; Wilson, 1987a). In many cases, the same statistic may reflect both progress and decline. How should these statistics, for example, be evaluated? In 1940, 5 percent of whites and 1 percent of blacks were college graduates. In 1985, the figures were 20 percent and 11 percent, respectively (Center for Education Statistics, 1987). The gap between the two groups was greater in 1985, but the ratio of progress was faster for African Americans than whites according to one criterion, greater distance according to the other. As Gunnar Myrdal suggested in 1962, the significance to Americans is often not some degree of change achieved but looking at the change in light of the general value of the American creed, the ideal. Nevertheless, the uneven distribution of diversity and the lack of progress, particularly with respect to some populations, is part of the concern expressed today.

Much of the early literature and research in higher education began from the assumption that the typical college student was white, was 18 to 24 years of age, lived in a residence hall, attended college full time, and was more often male than female. While a tendency remains to address questions as if these descriptors were still true, one would have a difficult time justifying such a description today. Tables 1 and 2 provide data on the enrollment characteristics of today's students, both graduate and undergraduate.

In fall 1985, 42 percent of all students were over 25, 52 percent were women, and 42 percent attended part time (Table 1). Women over 25 were 24 percent of all students enrolled in 1986 (O'Barr, 1989). In addition, in

TABLE 1
Higher Education Enrollments by Age, Gender, and Attendance Status, 1975 and 1985

	1975		1985		
	No.	Percent	No.	Percent	Change
Total	11,185		12,247		+9
14–24 years	7,061	63	7,151	58	+1
25 years and older	4,124	37	5,099	42	+24
Men	6,149	55	5,818	48	−5
Women	5,036	45	6,429	52	+28
Full time	6,841	61	7,075	58	+3
Part time	4,344	39	5,172	42	+19

SOURCE: Center for Education Statistics, 1987, p. 123.

TABLE 2
Higher Education Enrollments by Racial/Ethnic Group, 1976 and 1984

	1976		1984		
	No.	*Percent*	*No.*	*Percent*	*Change*
Total	10,986		12,163		+11
Hispanic	384	3.5	529	4.3	+38
White	9,076	82.6	9,767	80.3	+8
Black	1,033	9.4	1,070	8.8	+4
Asian/Pacific Islander	198	1.8	382	3.1	+93
Native American	76	0.7	83	0.7	+9
International	219	2.0	332	2.7	+52

SOURCE: Center for Education Statistics, 1987, p. 152.

1984 approximately 17 percent were members of an ethnic minority and another 3 percent were international students (Table 2).

The largest ethnic minority is African American, which in 1984 accounted for 8.8 percent of the total enrollment in higher education (Table 2). In that same year, African Americans made up 10.9 percent of the general population 18 years and older (Center for Education Statistics, 1986). Latinos were 4.3 percent of the enrollments in higher education, compared to 6.3 percent in the general population over 18. Asians were 3.1 percent compared to approximately 2 percent of the general population in 1980, and Native Americans accounted for less than 1 percent of the total enrollment and of the population in general (Carnegie Foundation, 1987; Chew and Ogi, 1987; Hsia, 1987).

While few data are available on the number of disabled students in higher education, current data suggest that from 3 to 6 percent of entering freshmen claim a physical disability of some sort (Astin, Green, and Korn, 1987; Fichten, 1986). It is more difficult to determine rates for learning disabilities given the problems of definition and the lack of systematic research on this topic in most national studies (Claxton and Murrell, 1987; Kirchner and Simon, 1984; Lopez and Clyde-Synder, 1983; Perry, 1981).

Taken as an aggregate, these figures represent a considerable change from 20 years ago. The number of African American students has more than doubled, and the representation of women, adult learners, and part-time students has increased considerably (Bean and Metzner, 1985; Blake, 1987; Lee, Rotermund, and Bertselman, 1985; Sedlacek and Webster, 1978). Today's overall enrollment figures in higher education do more adequately represent the patterns in the general population than they once did. Most of the changes, however, occurred during the late sixties and early seventies and reflect major efforts at the national, state, and local levels. The growth of the community college system, the move to a highly nonresidential and commuter student population, extensive federal and state financial aid programs, special services, and programmatic and curricular changes resulted in new populations of students. In particular, many authors cite financial aid as a key element in the change, particularly for minority populations (Astin, 1982; Bean and Metzner, 1985; Brown, Rosen, and Hill, 1980; Oliver and Etcheverry, 1987; Ostar, 1985; Stampen and Fenske, 1988; SHEEO, 1987).

Current and recent enrollment trends demonstrate that the thrust of those earlier changes has shifted. The progress in some cases has slowed and in others has been reversed. While Asian and Latino enrollments have increased both absolutely and as a percentage of the enrollment, African American enrollments declined between 1980 and 1984 despite increases in the high school completion rates of each group (Blake, 1987; Carnegie Foundation, 1987). Indeed, while the absolute and relative number of Latinos has increased, the increase is simply a function of the greater numbers graduating from high school rather than a function of an increased percentage going on to college. The proportion of African American and Latino young adults who are currently going on to college has declined in the 1980s (Carnegie Foundation, 1987; de los Santos, 1986; Wilson, 1987a, 1988). The general conclusion from this literature is that Latinos and Native Americans are still very much underrepresented. While the overall numbers for Asian students appear to be strong, the variation among Asian groups leaves some groups still underrepresented (Asian American Student Association, 1984; Hsia, 1988; SHEEO, 1987). In this instance, serious underlying issues become masked by grouping into one mass populations that are in truth quite different.

It must be recognized that the pattern of increases and declines in persons of color varies considerably from institution to institution. A 1987 study, for example, shows that while 20 percent of campuses reported increases in African American enrollments, 13 percent reported declines. The same is true for other ethnic groups, though many more campuses reported increases in Asian students (21 percent) than losses (7 percent) (El-Khawas, 1987; Lee, 1985).

While estimates of the disabled in the population vary, it appears that these students are still very underrepresented, although the absence of good information and basic definitions makes establishing a base of comparison very difficult (Asch, 1984; Jarrow, 1987; Marion and Iovacchini, 1983; Perry, 1981).

Distribution of Student Enrollments According to Institutional Type

The 3,000 institutions of higher education in this country have not been uniformly successful in achieving diversity as measured by student enrollments. Although historically African American institutions still enroll a disproportionate share of African American students in higher education, the great majority of African American students now attend traditionally white institutions (Allen, 1987; Livingston and Stewart, 1987; Morris, 1979; Wright, 1984). Most Native American students are enrolled in approximately 20 primarily Native American colleges, most of which are community colleges (Fries, 1987).

Table 3 illustrates the enrollment patterns for minority students between public and private institutions and between two- and four-year colleges and

TABLE 3
Total Enrollment by Race/Ethnicity of Student and Type of Institution, Fall 1984 (in Thousands)

	All Institutions No.	Public (Percent of Total)		Private (Percent of Total)	
		4-year	2-year	4-year	2-year
White	9,767	43	34	21	2
Black	1,070	40	39	18	4
Hispanic	529	33	53	12	2
Asian	382	41	42	16	1
Native American	83	36	51	10	4
Nonresident alien	332	51	15	33	1

SOURCE: Center for Education Statistics, 1987, p. 153.

universities. Among all college students, 77 percent attend public institutions and about 35 percent attend two-year public institutions. For Latino students, the figures are 86 percent in public institutions and 53 percent in two-year public institutions, for Asians 83 percent and 42 percent, and for Native Americans 87 percent and 51 percent. The most striking pattern to note is the high percentage of Latino and Native American students attending public two-year institutions. Because of the generally lower transfer and completion rates for two-year colleges, these figures have implications for retention and the completion of the baccalaureate degree (Arciniega, 1985; Mingle, 1987; Richardson and Bender, 1987; Turner, 1987).

Table 4 was prepared as the result of evidence indicating it is important to look at the differences between public and private institutions as well as different levels of institutions-universities, four-year colleges, and two-year colleges (Clowes, Hinkle, and Smart, 1986; Lee, 1985; Morris, 1979).

TABLE 4
Enrollment by Institutional Type and Race/Ethnicity, All Institutions, Fall 1984[a]

	All	White	Black	Hispanic	Asian	Native American	Foreign
Universities	24%	25%	13%	13%	24%	15%	42%
4-year	39%	40%	44%	32%	32%	30%	42%
2-year	37%	36%	43%	54%	43%	55%	16%
Universities							
Public	18%	19%	9%	9%	17%	13%	28%
Private	6%	6%	4%	4%	7%	2%	14%
4-year colleges							
Public	25%	24%	30%	24%	24%	23%	22%
Private	14%	15%	14%	8%	9%	7%	20%
2-year colleges							
Public	35%	34%	39%	53%	43%	51%	15%
Private	2%	2%	4%	1%	1%	4%	1%

[a]Totals may not be 100 as a result of rounding.
SOURCE: Center for Education Statistics, 1987, p. 153.

TABLE 5
Institutional Profile by Racial Enrollment, Universities, Fall 1984[a]

			4-Year		2-Year	
	Public	Private	Public	Private	Public	Private
Whites	85%	81%	79%	83%	78%	76%
Blacks	5%	6%	11%	8%	10%	16%
Hispanics	2%	3%	4%	3%	7%	4%
Asian	3%	4%	3%	2%	4%	1%
Native American	b	b	b	b	1%	1%
Foreign	4%	6%	2%	4%	1%	1%

[a]Totals may not be 100 as a result of rounding.
[b]Less than 1%.
SOURCE: Center for Education Statistics, 1987, p. 153.

This analysis separates the enrollment figures by level and by type of institution for students using fall 1984 enrollment figures. The data suggest that four-year institutions, particularly four-year public institutions, have the most even distribution of students across racial lines. While community colleges have a disproportionate share of minority enrollments, research universities have fewer minority members.

An alternative way to look at these figures is to compare minority distribution by type of institution. Table 5 illustrates that public four-year and public and private two-year institutions have the highest percentage of minority enrollments. The percentage of persons of color ranges from 24 percent in private two-year colleges to 15 percent in public universities. Once again, however, the pattern varies among ethnic groups. Latinos are most represented in public two-year institutions, African Americans in private two-year and public four-year institutions.

The status of overall enrollment demographics over the last 10 years suggests improvement in numbers for Asian students as a group and for women but less improvement, even loss, for Latinos and African Americans. It is also clear that students are clustered not only in various segments of the post-secondary system but also in various levels and fields within higher education. For example, the representation of women in the sciences and engineering has improved but is still very low. Moreover, the underrepresentation of African Americans, Latinos, and Native Americans in certain fields, such as the sciences, and at the graduate and professional levels is also apparent (Actin, 1982; Blackwell, 1988; Carnegie Foundation, 1987; Dix, 1987; Stern, 1988; Trent, 1984; Trent and Braddock, 1988). In general, the literature cites the issue of uneven distribution in fields for all minorities and for women. This underrepresentation has significant implications for the future of higher education and for society.

Enrollment Projections

Several possible scenarios can emerge from an analysis of the relationship between population demographics and patterns of college enrollment. One can assume, for example, that as the population in society diversifies, so too will the populations of colleges and universities. These projections are based on assumptions that the patterns of diversification will continue if only because the demographics of society are changing (Commission on Minority Participation, 1988; Estrada, 1988; Hodgkinson, 1985; Wilson, 1987a). Society is getting older, and more adults are expressing interest in furthering their education. Moreover, the ethnic makeup of precollegiate students reflects the increasingly diverse minority populations present in society. It is anticipated that by 2000, one-third of all school-age children will be members of ethnic minorities and that by 2010, one-third of the nation will be African American, Latino, Asian, or Native American (Commission on Minority Participation, 1988; Lee, 1985; Wilson, 1987b). Latinos alone are the second-largest and fastest-growing minority population in the United States (White and Sedlacek 1987). Moreover, it is likely that the disabled college population will also continue to grow as more differently abled students graduate from high school and efforts are intensified to provide access and support for them (Asch, 1984; California Community Colleges, 1986; Fichten, 1986; Hameister, 1984; Health Resource Center, 1987; Mick, 1985).

For this view to hold, institutional matriculation and success rates for the various subgroups in the population would have to be roughly equivalent. It also assumes that once arriving at the university, success rates would be roughly equal. This scenario is implicit in our assumptions about a desirable future. Certainly a review of today's enrollment patterns would support the view that this scenario has taken place in many institutions *to some degree and in some places.* Yet in some very important ways, it is not occurring. Enrollment patterns will not change simply because the population has changed.

A second view would predict that the demographic makeup within higher education will not reflect the changing character of the population and that a significant education gap will occur among groups in society. This scenario could emerge for a variety of different reasons. Differences in high school completion rates, differences in perception about the value of higher education, differences in institutional performance could all create this long-term picture. It is also possible that different subgroups of the population will not view higher education as capable of meeting their goals and will choose alternative routes for advancement (Arbeiter, 1987). The number of adults today attending alternative forms of postsecondary education and the larger number of minorities pursuing work and the military as alternatives to continued education give credence to this possibility (Cox and Jobe, 1988; Wilson, 1987b).

A third scenario would project dramatically uneven distributions of these various populations throughout postsecondary education, with some being educated at more selective colleges and universities and others being clustered in two-year institutions. While it may be the case that different institutions serve very different purposes and may thus serve certain populations better than others, distribution according to racial, gender, or age breakdowns raises serious questions for society. A policy analysis of the status of African Americans in higher education cautions (along with many others) that access cannot simply be evaluated across all of higher education (Morris, 1979). "Higher education in the United States has evolved into a highly refined institutional status hierarchy" (Actin, quoted in Morris, 1979, p. 56).

These three scenarios are all possibilities and to some degree are reflected in today's statistics. Thus, to the degree that each scenario is true today, the conclusion concerning higher education's success in achieving diversity in its enrollments is mixed (Chacon, Cohen, and Strover, 1986; El-Khawas, 1987; Hill, 1984; Richardson, Simmons, and de los Santos, 1987). Part of the concern expressed in the literature relates to the consequences that each scenario has for society.

> *In some way, our life as a nation depends both on cultivating intelligence to keep our complex social order running and preventing the formation of a permanently alienated, undereducated, unemployed, "underclass" (Bruner, 1983, p. 196).*

Retention

Retention is an important measure of success, but it is complicated by a variety of definitions and by the variety of ways in which it is measured. Institutional retention, for example, is a very important measure of success for institutions but, from the standpoint of public policy, may be less critical than retention as measured by completion of a degree. The general conclusions about retention in the literature emerge from a number of different sources. Some researchers have looked at the national rate of degree completion compared to enrollment to estimate retention rates (Commission on Minority Participation, 1988). Others have studied the retention rates of specific groups at the institutional level; still others have used such national data bases as the *Cooperative Institutional Research Project* or *High School and Beyond* to assess retention and degree completion (Hill, 1984; Hilton, 1986; Morris, 1979; Tinto, 1987). In general, the literature agrees that the overall retention of minorities, particularly African Americans, Latinos, and Native Americans, is lower than retention for white students and that overall retention is now about equal for men and women (Nettles, 1988b; SHEEO, 1987). The data on men and women overall and on men and women of color suggest that the timing of degree completion and the nature of the reasons when the degree is not completed differ (Tinto, 1987). Little data exist on retention as a function of age, though some data indicate that older students and other non-traditional students are more apt to leave for reasons external to the institution, such as jobs and family considerations, than would be true for traditional students (Bean and Metzner, 1985).

While most studies conclude that the rates of degree completion for African Americans, Latinos, and Native Americans are below that of whites and that the number of degrees conferred to African Americans has declined since 1975, the figures vary with the sample and measure being used (Blake, 1987; Cardoza, 1986; Commission on Minority Participation, 1988; Council of Graduate Schools, 1986; Hill, 1984; Hilton, 1986; Nettles, 1988a; Sanders, 1987; SHEEO, 1987; Sudarkasa, 1987; Webster, 1984; Wilson, 1987a, 1988). Nevertheless, many authors point with alarm to the dropout rates for these groups (Blake, 1987; Commission on Minority Participation, 1988; Sanders, 1987; Wilson, 1987a). One study estimates the rate of degree completion for whites to be two and one-half times the rate of degree completion for Latinos (Council of Graduate Schools, 1986), while another reports that the dropout rate for Native Americans is between 75 and 93 percent (Guyette and Heth, 1983). In any case, "a decline in educational attainment by any substantial population group is cause for deep concern" (Commission on Minority Participation, 1988, p. 14).

Again, types of institutions vary considerably. Some have pointed to the success of historically African American colleges and some of the more selective institutions in retaining and graduating minority students (Allen, 1987; Blake, 1987; Fleming, 1984; Gurin and Epps, 1975; Hart, 1984; Morris, 1979; Pascarella, 1985; Tinto, 1987). As stated earlier, historically African American colleges continue to account for a greater proportion of undergraduate and advanced degrees awarded to African Americans relative to the smaller proportion of African American students now attending historically African American colleges and universities (Hart, 1984; Morris, 1979; Nettles, 1988a; Richardson, Simmons, and de los Santos, 1987; Wilson, 1988). Some caution, however, that the picture is mixed at African American institutions (Nettles, Thoeny, and Gosman, 1986): Their recent studies have found that rates of progression are slower and rates of attrition are actually higher overall at African American institutions than at white institutions. Significant here are the background differences of students in attendance and whether the institution is public or private (Hartnett, 1970; Nettles, 1988b). African American institutions admit students who are less prepared by traditional standards and thus may be expected to have a higher rate of attrition. The data suggest that these institutions still graduate greater proportions of students than white institutions where the rate of attrition cannot be fully explained by academic preparation.

Some evidence also suggests that private institutions in general and African American private institutions in particular are more successful with regard to retention (Davis and Nettles, 1987; Hart, 1984; Hill, 1984; Nettles, Thoeny, and Gosman, 1987). Indeed, the proportion of degrees awarded to minorities in private institutions is twice that of public institutions (Richardson, Simmons, and de los Santos, 1987). These data are confounded by the heavy presence of minority students in public two-year institutions, where relatively few students move to four-year institutions (Chacon, Cohen, and Strover, 1986). Clearly, care must be exercised in making simple conclusions across institutions and institutional types. The interactions of race, gender, and institutional type and control are significant and can affect general conclusions about retention (Pascarella, 1985). Nevertheless, retention is a cause for national concern.

The Campus Environment: A "Chilly Climate"

Many campuses today look very different from 20 years ago, and a cursory glance might suggest that higher education has made significant progress in terms of students' diversity. But the challenge of diversity goes beyond the kinds of changes evidenced by increased programs and services. The consistent theme of alienation experienced by students of nontraditional backgrounds in their campus environments is symptomatic of a deep underlying problem that has not been adequately addressed. The voices of these students are those of people who feel like outsiders, "strangers in a strange land" (Beckham, 1988). The current literature suggests that some campus environments are more "chilly" than welcoming, more "alienating" than involving, more hostile than encouraging.

Again, it is important to recognize that generalizations across a complex and diverse system are risky. Information about students' experiences on their campuses, while significant, does not reflect the universal view of all students, nor does it reflect individual students' view of their campuses. One study of African American students at predominantly white institutions reports, for example, that their experiences were "not very unpleasant or very pleasant" (Allen, 1982), while a later work reports that experiences of racial discrimination were frequent (Allen, 1986). These mixed conclusions are not uncommon and may be related to degrees of association and to such factors as social distance (Carter and Sedlacek, 1984; Griffith, 1978; Loo and Robson, 1986; Lunneborg and Lunneborg, 1985; Patterson and Sedlacek, 1984; Peterson and Associates, 1978).

Although it is important to keep this perspective in mind, the following comment should nevertheless cause the higher education community to pause and reflect:

> *If a Rip Van Winkle who retired in 1966 came back today, resumed his reading of the* Chronicle of Higher Education, *and browsed through. . . . Change, he would have to wonder not at the magnitude of change since 1965 but at the continuity of problems. . . . The statistics for blacks are anything but cheering. . . . Yet perhaps the most conspicuous change a Rip would note is the deteriorated climate for interracial unity. . . . The presence of blacks in higher education falls woefully short of where men and women of good will hoped and trusted it would be by 1987 (Bornholdt, 1987, pp. 6–7).*

More sobering, this statement should not be read with only African American students in mind, because it could apply to virtually all nontraditional populations in one way or another. The literature reviewed through the following sections cites a myriad of barriers facing the diversity of students on their campuses, barriers that can be psychosocial, academic, financial, and physical. All too frequently, it mentions alienation (Asamen and Berry, 1987; Skinner and Richardson, 1988; Vasquez, 1982).

Women

The phrase "a chilly climate" was coined to reflect the experience of women on today's campuses for a report that says women, even though they constitute a majority of students, have not become fully integrated on today's campuses (Sandler and Hall, 1982). As other studies have suggested, the issues involved in women's achieving full integration concern not only numbers but also treatment by faculty, attitudes on campus about gender, curricula that still ignore the contributions of women, sexual harassment, the absence of role models, limited opportunities for leadership, and, even more fundamentally, approaches to learning that have not traditionally been reflected in the very value system of higher education (Belenky and Associates, 1986; Pearson, Shavlik, and Touchton, 1989; Sandler, 1987; Walton, 1986). Such research suggests that varieties of approaches to learning and inclinations toward cooperative learning styles, for example, are not easily accommodated on many campuses (Claxton and Murrell, 1987; Rossi, 1987; Sandler, 1987). The Carnegie Commission's recent study on the undergraduate experience (Boyer, 1986) reports that even today women are less likely to participate in class, and other studies support the conclusion (Krupnick, 1985).

If women, who constitute a majority of students and mirror their male counterparts in social, economic, and academic background, encounter a chilly climate on campus, how might persons of different ethnic and racial backgrounds or older students or the disabled perceive the campus? In general, the theme that emerges from research, interviews, and general commentary is that many campuses are alienating for their students (Beckham, 1988; Brown, 1982; Burrell, 1980; Elam, 1982; Freedman, 1981; McIntyre, 1981; Mallinckrodt and Sedlacek, 1987; Martin, 1985; Oliver and Associates, 1985; Parker, Scott, and Chambers, 1985; Ponterotto, Grieger, and Heaphy, 1985; Rasor, 1981; Suen, 1983; Zuber, 1981).

Minority Students

Because of increasingly focused concern about minority enrollments and retention, a reasonably large body of literature discusses the campus environment experienced by minority students. Because of their numbers in the population and their longer history in higher education, the experience of African American students provides the core of this literature (Allen, 1982, 1986; Elam, 1982; Loo and Rolison, 1986; Morris, 1979; Nettles, 1986; Patterson and Sedlacek, 1984; Peterson and Associates, 1978; Ponterotto, Grieger, and Heaphy, 1985). The amount of literature is growing on Latinos, particularly Chicanos, however, and literature on the experience of Asian and Native American students is emerging (Chacon, Cohen, and Strover, 1986; Hsia, 1988; Madrozo-Peterson and Rodriguez, 1978; Olivas, 1986; Oliver and Associates, 1985; Patterson, Sedlacek, and Perry, 1984; Rasor, 1981; Sanders, 1987;

Sue, 1981; Suen, 1983; Webster, 1984; White and Sedlacek, 1987). A forthcoming publication will address the chilly climate for women of color.

While a large component of this literature focuses on the needs of minority students that result from lack of adequate preparation in specific areas, financial pressures, or lack of support and advising, another phenomenon, not often addressed as directly, emerges from the literature. Study after study reports the experiences of minority students from all backgrounds who encounter racism and overt or subtle forms of discrimination by other students or faculty. Many of these students experience culture shock by being in an environment where dominant values, expectations, or experiences may be very different from their own and may be implicitly or explicitly devalued (Allen, 1982, 1986; Allen, Gurin, and Peterson, 1988; Asamen and Berry, 1987; Beckham, 1988; Chew and Ogi, 1987; Fiske, 1988; Garza and Nelson, 1973; Jaimes, 1980; Oliver and Associates, 1985; Parker, Scott, and Chambers, 1985; Sanders, 1987; Sedlacek, 1987; Sedlacek and Brooks, 1976; Wright, 1987; Zuber, 1981). While poor academic preparation and socioeconomic status may be a barrier to matriculation, evidence is growing that the poor quality of minority students' life on campus and their sense of isolation, alienation, and lack of support are more serious factors in attrition (Allen, 1988b; Armstrong-West and de la Teja, 1988; Bennett and Bean, 1983: Crosson, 1988; Jones, Harris, and Hand, 1975). One important factor associated with success for African American students is the degree of academic integration in campus life through the faculty and curriculum; on many campuses, integration is not sufficient in either academic or residential life (Nettles, Thoeny, and Gosman, 1986). How is one to be integrated in this kind of environment?

Ask a black student about the racial climate on campus and he or she will likely describe it as a microcosm of society. . . . They hear outlandishly insensitive statements and observe painful expressions of disrespect and downright hatred. Repeatedly, however, black experiences in mostly white colleges are chronicles of how the institutions have almost systematically bruised self-esteem and doled out mere pittances of support services (Beckham, 1988, p. 76).

The issues surrounding the campus environment go deeper than individual acts of overt racism to more subtle questions concerning values and customs. Native American students, for whom soft speech and indirect eye contact are appropriate behaviors, suffer the consequences when confronted with an environment in which argument, assertiveness, and directness may not only be expected but also viewed as indicators of intellect and academic commitment (Sanders, 1987). A comparison of perceptions of a university environment between Mexican American and Anglo-American students found significant differences between their perceptions and comfort with such things as politeness, assertiveness, and risk taking (Garza and Nelson, 1973). A number of studies on the learning styles of African American, Native American, and Latino youth suggest more variety than is usually dealt with in traditional forms of pedagogy (Claxton and Murrell, 1987). These patterns of difference reflect additional impediments to learning.

Research still suggests that white students have more negative attitudes toward African Americans, particularly in intimate or personal interactions, while African Americans are more likely to appreciate and value their interracial experiences (Carter, White, and Sedlacek, 1985; Carver, Glass, and Katz, 1978; Korolewicz and Korolewicz, 1985; Le Flore, 1982; Livingston and Stewart, 1987; Martinez and Sedlacek, 1983; Minatoya and Sedlacek, 1984; Switkin and Gynther, 1974). Ironically, despite common campus discussions about minority students who isolate themselves on campus, available research suggests that the amount of interracial contact among whites is much lower than it is for minorities (Dinka, Mazzella, and Pilant, 1980). Given the relatively small number of minorities on many campuses, these results are not surprising, suggesting that we need to be cautious about how we define the problem. In this case, the problem may not be minority students who isolate themselves but nonminorities who avoid contact. The rising number of reports about racial incidents on campuses across the country document a problem that appears to be increasing, one that reflects growing tension in dealing with diversity (Bechman, 1984; Rooks, 1988; Weinberg, 1982). A summary of the environment for racial and ethnic minorities on four-year campuses concludes that "while the scope and depth of racial and discriminatory attitudes and behavior are unknown, it is clear that many predominantly white four-year colleges and universities have somehow failed to live up to their ideals as civil and tolerant social communities that respect diversity and pluralism" (Crosson, 1988, p. 381).

The Adult Learner

Attendance at a college or university for adult learners often requires the juggling of many roles. These students often attend part time, hold jobs off campus, and have significant family commitments. At the same time, they are often very persistent and have clear goals for their education. Some, such as women reentering college, have been out of school a long time, and others face significant financial pressures as they struggle to get an education. When the adult learner is also a woman of color, the number of barriers is multiplied (Pearson, Shavlik, and Touchton, 1989). These factors provide challenges for both the student and the institution in terms of class schedules, child care, financial aid (which is often geared to the full-time student), career advisement, and access to the full range of services and programs. The student who cannot spend time on campus beyond the period spent in class cannot as easily learn about available services or how things are done or, indeed, experience the cultures of the campus itself. Many authors point out that the characteristics of the adult learner also have implications for methods of teaching and learning. Students expect that their academic program will not only acknowledge the validity of their own experiences but will also connect those experiences to their study. The literature suggests that the difference between the adult student and the traditional student presents significant challenges for teaching. The literature also describes the needs of adult students for emotional support and information (Bauer, 1981; Bodenkoop and Johansen, 1980; Courage, 1984; Creange, 1980; Duhon, 1986; Durnell, 1980; Hetherington and Hudson, 1981; Hu, 1985; Knowles, 1978; Saslow, 1981; Soldler, 1982).

Disabled Students

The passage of Section 504 of the Rehabilitation Act of 1973 not only has facilitated and encouraged the enrollment of students with physical and learning disabilities but also validated the legitimacy of concerns about access for those with disabilities.

The needs of these students, particularly those with physical disabilities, raise fundamental questions about access and accessibility on campuses. Through architectural modifications, the restructuring of testing procedures and curricular requirements, and the availability of interpreters, tape recorders, computer systems, and support services for the learning disabled, more campus programs have been made available. In many cases, these modifications have made learning more beneficial and fruitful for students, faculty, and staff whose own learning or physical needs do not classify them as disabled but who nevertheless have special needs.

The need to reduce barriers for these students appears relatively straightforward, although from an institutional point of view, it requires commitment and expense. The literature suggests, however, that the need for physical or curricular enhancements is not the most formidable barrier those with disabilities face. Studies report the social isolation of disabled students that results from the discomfort experienced by the nondisabled in their interaction with them. Professor Seymour Martin Lipset, a well-known sociologist, author of more than 40 books, and himself dyslexic, described the isolation for such students as "punishing" (*Stanford Observer* 1989, p. 6). Social isolation is pertinent, not only because of the obvious emotional consequences for the individual but also because it creates a loss of access to critical, albeit informal, information on how to succeed. In dealing with the issue of social isolation, the emphasis seems to be on educating the disabled person rather than educating the institution or the majority culture to include those students who are different. Indeed, one line of research focuses on techniques that disabled students can use to increase the comfort level of nondisabled students. Yet surveys suggest a preponderance of negative attitudes faced by the disabled, evidence of avoidance behavior, and discomfort, suggesting that the disabled raise issues of vulnerability to others (Asch, 1984; Belgrave, 1984; Demetrulias, Sattler, and Graham, 1982; Fenderson, 1984; Patterson, Sedlacek, and Scales, 1984; Richardson, 1976; Stilwell, Stilwell, and Perril, 1983; Yuker, Block, and Young, 1966).

Summary

The kinds of experiences reflected in the literature suggest the diverse populations of students we have been dealing with:

Have a wide variety of needs for specific programs and services;
Have powerful and alienating experiences with racism, discrimination, and stereotypic responses;
Have experienced campus attitudes and behaviors that isolate them;
Have experienced campuses that socially, physically, or programmatically (for example, through the curriculum) communicate to them that they do not belong or are not welcome;
Have experienced a campus culture and value system that may not be consistent with their own background;
Feel the pressure to be exemplary, a phenomenon that is particularly strong for members of visible minorities whose numbers are small in the institution.

These experiences include needs and barriers that are quite specific in focus and scope, such as ramps and tutorial programs. Others result simply from being different or being a member of a visible minority. These experiences can stem from behaviors and incidents that reflect insensitivity to issues of difference, but they can also result from the experience of feeling that one does not belong. Such feelings can be based on visual and physical cues in the environment, by simple observation of who is in charge, or by how one is treated.

The significance of the quality of the environment is very important. It may both directly and indirectly affect performance and persistence. Experiences of alienation, lack of comfort, and isolation not only deprive students of access to information, support, and programs but can also produce stress and a general lack of commitment that the rigors of an education necessarily require (Allen, 1988b; Etzioni, 1968; Maynard, 1980; Nettles, 1988a; Olivas, 1986; Rochin and de la Torres, 1987; Seeman, 1959; Uncapher and Associates, 1983; Zambrana, 1987). "While isolation can be detrimental, cross-cultural contacts can be especially damaging if members of the majority bring with them significant measures of prejudice, intolerance, ignorance, or disdain" (SHEEO, 1987, p. 33). If these issues are combined with deficits in academic preparation, the consequences of socioeconomic status, financial pressures, role conflicts, and family factors, it is not surprising that we see the negative figures related to retention and enrollment of groups different from the general population. These issues can be important for any member of the community who feels different but particularly for new students who at the same time are experiencing the transition to a new environment (Hall, 1984, 1986; Madden and Associates, 1987; SHEEO, 1987; Williams and Siegmar, 1978).

Deprivation has consequences for the rest of the community as well. The nontraditional student's lack of access to information and exchange results in lack of exchange for traditional students as well. It has long been argued that part of the reason students are required to learn other languages and about other cultures is that it broadens the student's understanding of society and how he or she is shaped by and in turn shapes the culture in which we live. The same reasoning applies to all aspects of diversity in an educational community (Bowser and Hunt, 1981; Katz and Ivey, 1977; Willie, 1981).

The Role of Student Characteristics

I N ATTEMPTING TO UNDERSTAND why some students succeed and others do not, research has focused on the role of background characteristics. Considerable caution must be exercised in interpreting the results of this approach. We are much clearer today that finding simple causal relationships is not possible. Moreover, by focusing attention on a narrow range of variables, we have restricted the investigation of other factors associated with success (Nettles, 1988b).

The classic literature on persistence and college performance has generally concluded that background characteristics are some of the most reliable predictors of success. High school grade point average, socioeconomic status, Scholastic Aptitude Test (SAT) scores, and parental education have continually emerged to predict persistence or college Grade Point Average (GPA) (Astin, 1975; Cope and Hannah, 1975; Pantages and Creedon, 1978). While most of that early literature did not differentiate among campus groups, except perhaps between men and women, the assumption remained that background characteristics were the most salient factors to look at to predict a student's success in college. Given that what is expected of a student in college is not unlike what is expected in high school, it is not unreasonable to pay serious attention to these factors. In coming to this conclusion, however, it is important to remember first that many of the early studies did not differentiate between voluntary and institutional dismissal. For some groups, academic background can play a more significant role in explaining academic failure. Second, while variables like high school GPA were often the largest predictors of persistence, they often accounted for only 10 to 12 percent of the variance in explaining persistence. In other words, academic background in many cases was not as potent an explanation of attrition as assumed (Tinto, 1987). Moreover, the tendency was to describe such variables as SAT scores and high school GPA as measures of academic ability rather than academic preparation or background, suggesting that the problem is innate as opposed to a function of experience.

While recent research still focuses on traditional students and traditional measures of academic preparation, a growing body of research looks at other factors associated with the success of a variety of nontraditional populations. Much of this research is finding that not only do factors related to academic preparation continue to be important but that other factors are also important (Arciniega, 1985; Astin, 1982; Bean and Metzner, 1985; Bennett and Okinaka, 1984; Burrell, 1980; Fields, 1988; Lynch, 1985; Nettles, 1988b). *Leaving College,* a very significant book, summarizes the most current literature on persistence, including a careful look at what can be said about retention for a variety of different populations, and cites the importance of differentiating between those who leave voluntarily and those who are dismissed for academic reasons (Tinto, 1987). It also points out the complex relationship between institutional characteristics and students' background characteristics as they relate to persistence. Using the National Longitudinal Study of the High School Class of 1972 as a base, Tinto points out that the differential in rates of persistence for African Americans can be traced more to educational background than to class or race but that this statement is not true for Latino students for whom persistence is not related to academic preparation but may be related more to their collegiate experience. The presence of greater numbers of Latino students in two-year institutions, where retention is lower, likely plays a role in their attrition.

In addition to traditional background characteristics, the literature reflects the importance of such factors as the commitment to academic or occupational goals, the quality of the student's effort, good study habits, attitudinal characteristics, and other kinds of life experience as related to success (Actin, 1975, 1985; DiCesare, Sedlacek, and Brooks, 1972; Fields, 1988; Nora, 1987; Pace, 1984; Wright and Associates, 1988). Important research has demonstrated the importance of noncognitive variables in predicting success (Sedlacek, 1982; Tracey and Sedlacek, 1984, 1985). This research comparing African American and white students concludes that noncognitive factors like positive self-confidence, understanding of racism, realistic self-appraisal, and community involvement are more significant than academic ability in predicting persistence. Another study found dropout rates for whites related to academic variables but for African Americans to a measure of social estrangement (Suen, 1983). As mentioned earlier, preparation cannot explain the high dropout rates for Latinos (Tinto, 1987). A very elegant study of Latinos in six community colleges found that commitment to the institution and to educational goals was an important indicator of retention (Nora, 1987). And evidence suggests that for many students, particularly commuter students, older students, and Chicanas, external factors like family and work demands play significant roles in persistence and performance (Actin and Burciaga, 1981; Bean and Metzner, 1985; Chacon, Cohen, and Strover, 1986; Zambrana, 1987).

Throughout this literature, the role of gender is dealt with unevenly. Nevertheless, the complex interaction between such characteristics as race and gender cannot be overlooked. Chicanas experience a different kind of stress as a function of family and work demands (Zambrana, 1987). An emerging theme in the literature concerns the declining presence of African American males in higher education (Wilson, 1988). Gender must be regarded as an important characteristic to be studied and understood along with race, culture, class, and disability (Bell-Scott, 1984; Pearson, Shavlik, and Touchton, 1989).

For all the years of research on the factors associated with persistence and performance, no clear answer exists to the question about the role of background characteristics. A danger is present, however, that the role of traditional measures of preparation continues to be overemphasized, thus overshadowing the role of the institution, the collegiate experience, and other noncognitive variables. For those already present in higher education, educational deficits may not be nearly as important as the deficits that emerge from lack of self-confidence and from being in environments that question one's presence there (Nettles, 1988b). While traditional forms of academic preparation cannot be ignored, these elements play more of a role for some students than for others, for some forms of withdrawal than for others, and in some institutional contexts than in others. In terms of students' characteristics, other noncognitive factors need to be understood, considered, and emphasized. Moreover, the institutional responsibility for these issues cannot be ignored. The institution, the situation, and the student all play roles in students' success.

The Challenge of Involvement

Theories of Involvement

Many recent national reports about higher education as well as studies of enrollment management have echoed a similar theme: the importance of students' involvement in their own learning process. Tinto (1987) and Astin (1975, 1985) among others have developed major theoretical positions and spawned significant research that stress the importance of students' involvement in the academic enterprise. Both point out that the role of involvement can be both direct and indirect. Clearly, students are more apt to learn and to succeed if they are involved in their courses and involved with the curriculum. But research also shows that being involved with one's peers, with faculty outside the classroom, and with the institution can also facilitate success (Astin, 1985; Fox, 1985; Nettles and Johnson, 1987; Pascarella, 1980; Rooney, 1985). Connections of this sort not only create a comfort level with the environment and offer academic and emotional support; they also provide access to information that facilitates adaptation to academic life beyond what is presented in handbooks and catalogs. Access to information has been cited as critically important to a number of nontraditional groups, particularly those who are part time and those who commute. Such students are especially vulnerable to the complications that come from "not knowing" (Creange, 1980; Hetherington and Hudson, 1981; Hu, 1985; Nora, 1987; Vaz, 1987).

Tinto has developed a model of retention that has evolved from earlier models of student outcomes. His work is more explicit, however, in describing the complex interactions between background characteristics and the campus environment, positing that the fit between the student and the environment involves both social and academic integration in the institution. *Social integration* relates to involvement with peers, campus activities, and so on, while *academic integration* relates to academic performance, involvement with the curriculum, and contact with faculty and staff. Tinto suggests that when a student experiences integration, that student is more likely to persist. Importantly, lack of fit—or incongruence—occurs when the individual views himself or herself "at odds with the institution," a phrase that comes very close to describing the concept of alienation (Babbit, Bruback, and Thompson, 1975; Braddock, 1978; Loo and Rolison, 1986).

A student's involvement—or lack of it—can be with different parts of the institution and can vary by degree. Clearly, most institutions are comprised of any number of complex subcultures with which an individual might identify. Moreover, certain kinds of campuses, such as small institutions or residential campuses, may provide more opportunity for involvement than others. Based on his summary of the literature, Tinto suggests that centrality of the group is also an important factor; that is, the degree to which the group with which one identifies is perceived as being central to the institution is an important element fostering feelings of involvement with that institution. He cites some literature suggesting that the most effective support programs for minorities, for example, are those perceived to be central rather than peripheral to the institution. The implications are important. In particular, it might not be sufficient for an individual student to be involved with just any group if he or she perceives that that group is marginal to the institution.

A reasonable amount of research now supports Tinto's model. Some of the work investigating the different forms of integration—academic or social, informal or formal—suggests that one or the other might be more important for different groups under different circumstances. Not surprisingly, the results are not entirely consistent, suggesting that many factors are related to the significance of involvement. One study found that dropout behavior for African American students was related to social estrangement (Suen, 1983), and a study of African American and white men and women found that social integration is more important for African American men, that both academic and social integration are significant for African American women, and that academic integration is most important for whites (Stoecker, Pascarella, and Wolfe, 1988).

These factors of race and gender may also interact with the type of institution. For African American students at historically African American colleges, academic integration appears to relate to success, whereas some have found that social integration is more important at traditionally white institutions for African American males (Pascarella, 1985). Other research suggests, however, that the danger of too much social integration and not enough academic integration can be a negative factor for African American men at white institutions (Nettles, Thoeny, and Gosman, 1987). Others have found that black colleges tend to achieve greater academic integration for both African American and white students, including greater involvement on the part of African American and white faculty in the lives of students (Allen, 1987; Fleming, 1984; Gurin and Epps, 1975; Nettles, Thoeny, and Gosman, 1987). A study of Latinos in six community colleges found that educational goals and institutional commitment were mediated by factors of involvement (Nora, 1987).

Astin has also emphasized the importance of involvement to academic success. By building on research related to learning theory, earlier studies involving the quality of effort (Pace, 1984), and his own work, Astin concludes that involvement in learning and involvement in campus life are critical factors in institutions' and students' success. By involvement, he means the "amount of physical and psychological energy that the student devotes to the academic experience" (Astin, 1985, p. 36). The implication is that the effectiveness of any program can be assessed by the quality and degree of students' involvement.

Astin suggests, however, that the goal of involvement is often difficult to accomplish, because some fundamental values within academic life run counter to it. The lack of progress in improving learning can partly be ascribed to a basic conflict between deep values rooted in the academic tradition and the conditions that tend to promote success and learning. It is now understood that learning and the commitment to learning are best accomplished in an environment of cooperation and support and that such an environment is most likely to promote involvement. Competition, which has been so important to many campuses, is increasingly being recognized as detrimental for many students (Astin, 1987; Belenky and Associates, 1986; Martin, 1985; Palmer, 1987; Sanders, 1987; Sandler, 1987; Sandler and Hall, 1982). Grading on a curve, for example, is problematic because it puts people in comparison with one another, with the success of a few serving to impede the success of others. Universal success is impossible when using such a curve. This structure reinforces a competitive environment that is facilitated by the need and desire of today's students to succeed (Astin, 1987). Indeed, faculty who create alternative structures in which all students can succeed have been accused of contributing to grade inflation and have frequently been soundly criticized for their approaches.

The research to date has been unusually successful in supporting the importance of integration and involvement as important factors in persistence and success. While much work needs to be done in understanding the nature and importance of involvement for nontraditional groups, the research here also suggests the significance of the concept. In light of it, earlier descriptions of noninvolvement and alienation become particularly significant. We find evidence of noninvolvement—indeed alienation—on campuses for many nontraditional students. Such findings may help explain why so many students do not perform up to their potential.

The sources of the alienation may originate from a variety of experiences, ranging from racial discrimination to a sense of "not belonging." Some of the alienation may also be attributed to the presence of certain values in the institution that conflict with an individual's own patterns of learning or culture. Competition, which can be antithetical to learning for anyone, may be particularly difficult for groups whose own cultures emphasize cooperation. If the challenge of diversity is to be met, campuses must confront these issues.

Being the other is feeling different, is awareness of being distinct, is consciousness of being dissimilar. It means being outside the game, outside the circle, outside the set. Otherness results in feeling excluded, closed out, precluded, even disdained and scorned. It produces a sense of isolation, of apartness, of disconnectedness, of alienation (Madrid, 1988, p. 2).

In contemporary higher education, the condition of diversity is all too often a condition of alienation. If the theories and research on the central importance of involvement are true, these conditions must change. Several bodies of literature outside higher education add perspective to understanding the complexity of the challenge of involving students of diverse backgrounds in our institutions. The literatures on cultural pluralism, intergroup relations, and demography suggest important elements to be considered.

Cultural Pluralism

If institutions are to meet the challenge of diversity and create campuses in which students are truly involved, it is clear that how we conceive of the institution needs to be clarified. Despite the discussions about increasing diversity in the student body, the underlying assumption in much of the literature has appeared to be that the goal for students is assimilation into the dominant values and characteristics of the university (Blackwell, 1987; Hunt, 1975). Indeed, some observers believe that the groups most successful in integrating into American society and education have been those whose own backgrounds were closest to the dominant European traditions in the culture or those who gave up their identities to be "Americanized" (Castaneda, 1974; Gordon, 1964; Peterson and Associates, 1978; Rokeach, 1972; Sue, 1981). Whether assimilation is an appropriate goal and if so to what norm one should assimilate are important questions at the forefront of the issue of diversity today. For women, "assimilation has been viewed as the path to equality. . . . [but] assimilation at the expense of femaleness becomes not only undesirable but a kind of death" (Desjardins, 1989, p. 144). Many who struggle with what it means to be different have echoed such a view.

In contrast to the notion of assimilation, the term "cultural pluralism" has emerged to signify a society and community in which diversity is valued and in which difference can coexist with the concept of community (Astin, 1984; McBay, 1986; Terry, 1981).

The literature includes many different metaphors and models for cultural pluralism and reflects some underlying contradictions in our understanding of pluralism and our language for it (Banks, 1981; Quevedo-Garcia, 1987). Moreover, the view of what a culturally pluralistic society looks like varies. The cultural separatist provides for the maintenance of separate cultures that coexist as long as one group does not infringe on the rights of another, and the emphasis is on cultural preservation. The cultural diffusion model suggests that interaction among groups, interethnic social relationships, and the borrowing of traditions will occur. Some who propose this model as the ideal also maintain that because the Anglo-American tradition is dominant in this culture, everyone must acquire certain of the traits associated with it to succeed. This view suggests a bicultural model in which the dominant culture does not change but the individuals become facile in moving between their personal culture and the culture of the society. A third model describes cultural fusion in which diverse cultures come together to form a new culture that reflects and integrates the best of many cultures (Watson, 1980).

A pluralistic approach acknowledges and stresses ethnic or group identity (Hunt, 1975). A recent report on the racial climate at MIT defines pluralism as "a social condition . . . in which several distinct ethnic, religious, and racial communities live side by side, willing to affirm each other's dignity, ready to benefit from each other's experiences, and quick to acknowledge each other's contributions to the common welfare" (McBay, 1986, p. 2). A thoughtful analysis of the concept of cultural pluralism suggests that several problems are involved with proposing the model of cultural pluralism without addressing some of its limits (Suzuki, 1984). As defined by MIT, for example, cultural pluralism adopts a kind of federalist approach to diversity that focuses on the distinctiveness of each group without acknowledging any unifying values or goals. This idealized model, however, suggests that by allowing for group identity, issues of racism, sexism, classism, or homophobia will disappear, an assumption that is not likely to be valid. It also does not reflect the need to deal with the conflict that will inevitably result. The needs of the group may conflict with those of the larger community or other groups, and such conflicts must be resolved. One of Suzuki's most challenging reflections is that the existing social structure, particularly large centralized bureaucracies, may make the achievement of true cultural pluralism impossible. The idea of communities living "side by side" reflects some degree of autonomy and self-control in matters that our large public bureaucracies make very difficult (Suzuki, 1984).

A creative tension clearly exists between the call for involvement and the call for pluralism. Involvement in the institution suggests the ability to share certain values or goals, while pluralism leaves open the possibility of living parallel but separate lives. It would appear that the challenge is to try to define values in which people can share but that at the same time allow for important differences to be acknowledged, even nourished. Rather than similarity, diversity, whether in technology, geography, religion, or origins, is the natural order of things, and the founding values of this country were based on shared values about diversity, requiring the resolution of issues of community versus individual rights (Madrid, 1988). This tension is certainly apparent in the U.S. Constitution with respect to matters of state and federal jurisdiction. It also appears in higher education literature, where a creative tension exists between those who argue for the importance of academic freedom and creative anarchy and those who argue for the importance of shared values and organizational culture (Clark, 1972; Masland, 1985; Weick, 1976).

Resolving these tensions requires reflectiveness about institutional goals and values and about the ways in which "shared values" on the one hand and the "value of diversity" on the other can be brought together. Such an effort is complicated by the impact that power differentials, inequality, and past experiences have on institutional discussions. And being in a minority or majority position changes the way one approaches these questions (Wilkerson, 1989).

It also requires an acknowledgment that conflicts will emerge and that institutions that are prepared for the challenge of diversity will also be prepared for conflict and thus will have the means for resolving conflicts. If the challenge of a pluralistic institution is to create a process where each student will experience an environment that accepts his or her preferred modes of relating, communicating, and learning as equally important (Castaneda, 1974), then the challenges to higher education cannot be underestimated, particularly in large bureaucratic structures where multiple choice tests, large lecture halls, and little interaction may be the prevailing modes. Such a model also presupposes knowledge and respect and a desire to learn among each of these groups and the institution.

Intergroup Relations

A long tradition of research and scholarship has grown out of concern for furthering interracial cooperation in this country. The dominant questions have centered on the characteristics that would promote harmony among groups (Allport, 1954; Pettigrew, 1985). In light of the challenges of diversity, this literature contributes significant perspectives. "Intergroup relations represent in their enormous scope one of the most difficult and complex knots of problems [that] we confront in our time" (Tajfel, 1982, p. 1). The early assumptions had been that simply promoting contact among people would improve relationships. The now-classic *Nature of Prejudice* points out that simple proximity among people of different backgrounds is not enough and began to try to specify conditions under which such interactions would be positive (Allport, 1954). It concludes that these interactions would be successful only if those involved possess equal status, seek common goals, depend cooperatively on one another, and interact with the positive support of authorities, laws, and customs. Nevertheless, achieving cooperation among groups is difficult because a pattern of favoritism develops among members of the same group. Any tendencies to categorize people naturally leads to an in-group, out-group division in which members of one's own group are inclined to be favored, particularly in a context of conflict or when the status of different groups differs (Konrad and Gutek, 1987). As a result, simple proximity of individuals will not produce the kind of involvement and interaction one would hope for. It also appears that it is difficult to stop people from making categorical divisions. Simply placing people into groups tends to enhance the view that they are significantly different. In the case of visible minorities, women, the physically disabled, or older students, it may not be possible to avoid such categorizations. Thus, those who argue that institutions should not focus on the diversity within the campus may be ignoring the reality that such divisions will occur.

Certain conditions may *increase* intergroup tension and prejudice:

1. When the contact produces competition;
2. When the contact is unpleasant and involuntary;
3. When the prestige or status of one group is lowered as a result of contact;
4. When members of a group or the group as a whole are in a state of frustration;
5. When the groups have moral or ethical standards objectionable to the other;
6. When the minority is of lower status or lower in any relevant characteristic (Amir, 1969, pp. 338–339).

The conditions for conflict rather than cooperation among groups are clearly present on many campuses (Epps, 1974). Nevertheless, this literature has also begun to point out to organizations the benefits of facing these challenges rather than viewing them as a complication. A recent review of the literature suggests that the negative impact of this pattern of discrimination between groups can be reduced by stressing cooperation among groups, by encouraging contact between groups based on true equality, and by facilitating membership in several groups (Tajfel, 1982). This last item has important significance in this area. Theoretically, individuals who hold memberships in several groups begin to break down the rigid notions of "in" group and "out" group that form the basis of tensions and stereotyping among groups. By participating in both, they facilitate the reduction of stereotyping within either group. The support of policies, procedures, and customs is also critical (Asch, 1984; Tajfel, 1982).

One conclusion to be drawn from this literature is that simple proximity is not enough. Proximity creates potential, but it does not necessarily promote the kinds of goals for involvement that are central to a quality education (Johnson, Johnson, and Mariyama, 1983). Moreover, when individuals of differing status come together without appropriate support and without mutually beneficial tasks, the climate may be negative. Institutions addressing the challenge of diversity need to address issues of status groupings, institutional support and climate, membership in several groups, and significant contact in which the task is functionally important. The nature of many of today's institutions, combined with increasing enrollments of students of many different kinds of backgrounds, may explain some of the tension occurring today on college campuses.

Demography

While the phrase "changing demographics" found today in the literature of higher education is taken to mean changing numbers of different populations of students, the study of demographics can provide important perspectives on how organizations will function. The demography of an organization refers to its composition in terms of basic attributes like age, sex, educational level, and length of employment.

At its most basic, organizational demographics focuses on the significance of numbers. It is argued that the composition of an organization broadly affects institutional characteristics like interpersonal and intergroup interaction, morale, turnover, and performance. Kanter (1977) describes in great detail the ways in which proportional representation of groups can affect how people in an organization relate to one another, in particular focusing on the significance of being the only one, or the token member, of any visible minority. In many ways, what she describes is a no-win situation in which members of the minority or the majority will not find a comfortable way of relating.

When a group achieves 20 percent of a population, issues of tokenism appear to decrease. Groups of individuals who hold smaller proportions are vulnerable to increased visibility, scrutiny, and pressure, which can result in reduced performance and increased psychological stress (Kanter, 1977; Mingle, 1987; Pfeffer, 1983, 1985). Extreme tokenism, being the only one of a group, may also promote a conservatism that does not at all reflect diversity; that is, the individual is under pressure to look and act like the majority if she or he is to succeed. Of course, it is done at a significant cost to the person's own integrity and sense of effectiveness (Martin, 1985; Sandler, 1987).

A set of apparently contradictory consequences occur when one describes the condition of being in the minority, and these conditions seem to exist simultaneously. The first is that being in such a position has benefits and disadvantages (Konrad and Gutek, 1987; Phillips and Blumberg, 1982). A visible minority invariably becomes the focus of attention and as such might benefit from being noticed. At the same time, being the focus of attention means one comes under greater scrutiny and stress. Being "'the other' is invisible" while at the same time "sticking out like a sore thumb" (Madrid, 1988).

The impact of different proportions also is somewhat contradictory. Theoretically, as the numbers of minorities increase, more opportunities should exist for contact and the breaking down of stereotypes. But some evidence indicates that as numbers increase, the majority group becomes more threatened, particularly when persons of differential status are involved. It may be that as numbers increase, it is more comfortable for minorities but less comfortable, at least for a period, for the majority (Kanter, 1977; Konrad and Gutek, 1987; Kraiger and Ford, 1985; Loo and Rolison, 1986).

The literature on campus environments provides some support for these propositions and their apparent contradictions. With the exception of women and adult learners, most groups under discussion here constitute a minority at the present time. All ethnic minorities combined still constitute less than 20 percent of the enrollment in higher education. The issue of tokenism therefore remains central even when individual minority groups are blended together. When these groups are viewed separately, issues of tokenism become even more evident.

Summary

While it is challenging to draw conclusions from such a wide-ranging array of theory and research as presented in the literatures on involvement, demography, pluralism, and intergroup relations, we can conclude that:

1. Involvement and integration—formal or informal, academic or social— are critical elements for success. The literatures on academic integration and intergroup relations support the importance of involvement.

2. While an institution can assume that creating formal and informal opportunities for involvement is important, we need to pay careful attention to whether the forms of that involvement will be different for different groups and individuals. African Americans and Chicanos may experience such efforts differently from international students or recent immigrant groups. Furthermore, it must be recognized that variations across different kinds of institutions will exist as well. What can or will work at one place may not work at another.

3. Highly competitive environments may be detrimental not only to learning but also to creating opportunities for collaboration and memberships in several groups so important for pluralistic communities.

4. Centrality is a key dimension as one evaluates participation and programs. Involvement is more significant when it is closer to the center of rather than peripheral to the institution's mission. Institutions must pay attention to the ways in which students are encouraged to become involved and the ways in which those students *perceive* the forms of involvement. The higher

education community has talked about the importance of diversity for some years, but without visible and tangible signs of that centrality, others may not perceive the message.

5. Having significant enough numbers in a group helps provide the variety and "critical mass" to reduce the consequences of tokenism. A figure of 20 percent is often mentioned as a critical point. But having sufficient numbers and proportions is not enough. Without sufficient numbers, efforts at creating communities that are comfortable with diversity will be difficult. Having sufficient numbers does not guarantee a successful educational experience.

6. Being a member of a nontraditional population is all too often synonymous with alienation. If involvement and integration are essential ingredients for success, this connection must be broken.

7. The literature on intergroup relations suggests that simple contact among diverse groups will not in itself create an environment that values diversity. Factors such as unequal status, perceived lack of institutional support, a competitive climate, and lack of significant common tasks can lead to conflict and frustration.

8. Students will do better in environments that are open, accepting, and affirming. Efforts to establish cooperation and trust are critical to creating environments in which students can be involved. Such efforts, however, raise questions of institutional, group, and individual values that may need to be addressed if a connection between the institution and its students is to be firmly established. Creating environments that are open in these ways will sometimes confront the behaviors and attitudes of the majority.

9. Institutions will need to discuss the meaning of pluralism, those values for which the institution stands, and those values around which differences can exist.

10. Institutions will need to know much more about students, groups, and institutional processes. Demographic information on the institution, perceptions about the environment, data on the group affiliations of students, and the degree of interaction among students and student groups can be essential.

11. Institutions need to be sensitive to the difficult role of those in token positions (whether intentional or not) and to some of the inevitable strains it will create.

12. Conflict will be an inevitable part of the process of creating educational communities in a pluralistic context. In addition, some of the conditions for intergoup tension (unequal status, lack of shared tasks, and so on) are present on many campuses today.

The research on involvement and intergroup relations calls for greater opportunities for cooperative tasks. The literatures on cultural pluralism and demography point out the ways in which creating such opportunities will be difficult. The challenge of diversity rests on meeting the objectives of involvement along with and perhaps through pluralism. The classic work, *The Impact of College on Students,* describes the kinds of colleges and universities with the greatest potential for educational impact as those with a clear sense of mission and students from diverse backgrounds (Feldman and Newcomb, 1969). Such institutions may be the most successful in creating involvement through the kind of commitment to shared purposes that Allport describes. At the same time, the diversity of backgrounds contributes varieties of perspectives to the questions at hand. Institutions with numbers of diverse populations but no sense of shared purposes may invite attrition because no one feels involved in the institution. Overly homogeneous institutions may have a difficult time facilitating learning. In this context, diversity can be viewed as an essential element to the creation of a truly educational community.

Institutional Responses to Diversity

Approaches of Successful Institutions

Some striking similarities occur in the conclusions of many studies that have looked at "successful" institutions, even when a variety of student populations are being considered. Many focus on the need to develop strong programmatic responses that attempt to facilitate academic and social integration and are therefore quite consistent with the theories of involvement. In general, these institutions concentrate on five areas:

1. *Providing students with the tools to succeed.* At successful institutions, student assistance is viewed as comprehensive and central to the institution, and the quality of instruction is a high priority. Students are therefore free to take advantage of all resources without stigma. In addition to academic support services, financial assistance, tutoring, and technical support, such programs also focus on intensive advising programs that use faculty and students as mentors and follow up through the monitoring and evaluation of students' progress (Blake, 1987; Cardoza, 1986; Gittell, 1985; Glennen, Boxley, and Farren, 1985; Richardson and de los Santos, 1988; Valencia Community College, 1981).

2. *Developing increased coordination with the sector involving kindergarten through grade 12 and articulation between sectors.* Early academic preparation and the development of long-term educational goals are important factors in matriculation. As a result, successful institutions have begun to develop programs with elementary and secondary schools to assist in the process of

identifying students who aspire to college, helping students set goals, educating counselors, and working with teachers (Blakely, 1987; Nelms, 1982; Richardson and de los Santos, 1988; SHEEO, 1987). In addition, such institutions recognize that many nontraditional students begin their college careers in community colleges. Articulation programs, counseling, data collection, appropriate curricula, and financial assistance are all important features of efforts to facilitate and encourage the transition among sectors of higher education (Mingle, 1987; Richardson and Bender, 1987).

3. *Creating an "accepting" campus climate or an "academic environment that nourishes and encourages students to succeed"* (Commission on Minority Participation, 1988; Rendon and Nora, 1988; Shavlik, Touchton, and Pearson, 1989). These efforts invariably move beyond a focus directed simply toward students and their needs to acknowledging the role of institutional policies, procedures, and programs in affecting the creation of a positive climate for diversity. These efforts inevitably include all members of the campus community, and central to them are the diversification of the curriculum, faculty, and staff, the addition of policies and procedures that attempt to ensure that appropriate values and standards of expected behavior are clear and diligently enforced, and the creation of personal and programmatic support systems that encourage involvement and success at all levels.

4. *Developing access to adequate information* and a good database that focuses on students, the barriers they face, and the factors associated with successful completion of their programs. Because of the obvious diversity in the needs of different students and the diversity in campus structures and mission, each institution monitors itself and its students.

5. *Providing strong and focused leadership.* The importance of campus leadership is often mentioned as critical to whatever institutional efforts are made. Effective leadership from the faculty and administration helps to create an institutional agenda and to convey the significance of the efforts. Strong institutional statements may also help alleviate some of the risk often taken by those who are in the minority when they speak out on institutional and curricular matters (Carodo and Mangano, 1982; Clewell and Ficklen, 1986; Gittell, 1985; Goldberg and Associates, 1985; Hu, 1985; Lang, 1987; Larwood, Gutek, and Gattiker, 1984; Neher, 1985; Parker, Scott, and Chambers, 1985;

Peterson and Associates, 1978; Roueche and Baker, 1987; Shavlik, Touchton, and Pearson, 1989; Soldler, 1982; Spaights, Dixon, and Nicholas, 1985).

Lessons from the Women's Colleges

No single sector of higher education has been able to respond fully to all aspects of the diversity that is discussed here. Lessons can be learned, however, from institutions whose missions are dedicated to one or the other groups under consideration. These environments make explicit the support for their constituency, providing a de facto statement of the priority given this goal in all that the institution does. Whether the institution is a Gallaudet University dedicated to deaf students, a historically African American college, a college dedicated to Native Americans, or a women's college, these institutions are important. To the degree that they are special, they can be models for other institutions of what is needed if one is to create institutions truly dedicated to educating the diversity of students today. The literatures on women's colleges and historically African American institutions were reviewed for this purpose. These literatures also point to the barriers that these institutions face in their goals to educate particular populations.

Observers generally agree that women's colleges, even while controlling for selectivity, have in the past graduated and continue to graduate a greater percentage of women achievers than comparable coeducational colleges (Oates and Williamson, 1978; Rice and Hemmings, 1988; Tidball, 1988). Many of the writers involved engage in discussion and debate about the factors associated with this success and in particular whether it is a function of the institution or the kind of student who attends. Some have attributed it less to the environment and programs of these colleges than to the kinds of students who have attended (Oates and Williamson, 1978). Indeed, it is difficult to sort out all these relationships and to establish clear cause-and-effect relationships among such things as selectivity, environment, and success. Nevertheless, agreement is general about what graduates of women's colleges have achieved, the level of students' satisfaction, and the kind of climate created (Rice and Hemmings, 1988).

Women's colleges—those that are historically African American and those that are predominantly white—have been able to provide an environment in which women are seen as central and in which women are present in diverse roles throughout the faculty and staff. Only in women's colleges does anything close to equity exist in terms of faculty status, membership, and rank, and it is from the women's colleges that the vast majority of women college presidents come ("The College President," 1988; Simmons, 1978; Women's College Coalition, 1981).

Some have demonstrated a remarkably high correlation between the proportion of women on the faculty and the rate of women achievers in those institutions, leading to the conclusion that the presence of women on the faculty is one of the most important factors in women's achievement (Tidball, 1973, 1976, 1980). Even those who believe that not enough consideration is given to students' entering characteristics have concurred with the importance of this factor and an environment that speaks to women's specialness and capacity for success (Oates and Williamson, 1978).

Women's colleges have not always been leaders in curricular innovation out of fear of having their curricula negatively compared to traditional institutions. Even so, their curricula and teaching have been more apt to reflect women's concerns, simply because they were more likely to be taught by and to women (Stimpson, 1987). Moreover, evidence suggests that male faculty at women's colleges also explicitly support the goals of women's education (Women's College Coalition, 1981). In addition, the environment of women's colleges challenges women to become all those things they are not asked to be in many "coeducational" environments. They are faculty and student leaders, chairs of committees, merit award recipients, mentors, and beneficiaries of mentors. The environment of these colleges provides opportunities for varieties of leadership styles, for success and failure, and for nonstereotypic approaches to women and "their" issues. Research conducted even in recent years points out that women behave differently and are treated differently when they are in all-female environments than when they are in coed groups or when they are taught by women rather than by men (Krupnick, 1985).

Because of the same attitudes that often confront women concerning their value or importance, women's colleges have to deal with society's perceptions and often feel they have to take a conservative approach with respect to women's education to prove their value. Many also have been on the defensive about their successes. The result has been that fewer of these institutions are left to provide models of what institutions dedicated to women can mean.

Lessons from the Historically African American Institutions

While one can debate the role of selectivity in explaining the rates of achievement for graduates of women's colleges, this issue is not as much of a factor in discussing the achievement of the historically African American colleges, particularly in recent years. Known for educating students with wide-ranging academic backgrounds, these institutions are further challenged by fewer resources than other institutions and increasing competition for their students. Nevertheless, these institutions account for a much greater share of African American degrees at all levels than their enrollments would account for and have demonstrated success for a broader range of students than have traditionally white institutions (Cross and Actin, 1981; Fleming, 1984; Green, 1989; Gurin and Epps, 1975; Hart, 1984; McClain, 1979; Maryland State Board, 1981; Smith, 1981; Wilson, 1988).

One analysis of the rate of degrees completed suggests clearly that traditionally African American institutions, along with some selective northeastern universities, have had the most success in terms of graduation rates (Hart, 1984). The ACE's recent handbook supports this analysis, noting that in 1984–85 they awarded 34 percent of the BA degrees while enrolling only 18 percent of African American students (Green, 1989). In addition, 50 percent of the African American faculty in white research universities received their undergraduate degrees at historically African American colleges and universities (Wilson, 1988).

The literature contains considerable disagreement about other benefits of attending either white or African American institutions. These studies rely heavily on statistical data, but the approaches and the sources of data yield different conclusions. Researchers, many employing multivariate statistical techniques, have looked at whether institutional type makes a significant difference when such factors as background characteristics are controlled. The results are mixed. A study of African American students at both white and African American institutions found greater cognitive development and higher aspirations among African American students attending African American institutions

(Fleming, 1984). It also noted that African American women become more assertive at white institutions. Another researcher has not found institutional type in general to be a predictor of success (Pascarella, 1985). Some have found mixed benefits from attending traditionally African American or white institutions in terms of speed of completion and performance (Nettles, 1988a). For example, one study found that African American students are more likely to complete the degree in four years at a traditionally African American institution but may have some career advantages if they attend a traditionally white institution, presumably because of the access to "the mainstream" (Braddock and McPartland, 1988). The conclusions from this kind of research go to the heart of concerns about society, because they suggest that success in a career may be related to having access to people in power and that such access may be more readily available in traditionally white institutions.

The evidence suggests that the impact of attending one kind of institution over the other varies with the particular nature of the institution and its resources, the particular student involved, and other factors, such as gender (Allen, 1988b; Fleming, 1984; Pascarella, Smart, and Stoecker, 1989). Numbers of authors point to the sometimes difficult choices that students are asked to make between access to prestige and resources against access to personal growth and satisfaction (Allen, 1988b). They generally agree, however, that historically African American colleges and universities succeed in involving students academically as well as providing environments that make their success a central part of the institution's mission. These institutions accommodate both educational equity and intellectual development in a common mission. Authors point to the generally positive climate in these institutions, taking the form of wider networks of friendship, more opportunities for involvement, and greater expectations for success (Allen, 1988b; Fleming, 1984; Gillespie, 1983; Gurin and Epps, 1975; Morris, 1979; Nettles,1986; SHEEO, 1987). Historically African American colleges have served and continue to serve an important role in higher education by providing the bulk of African American leadership and advanced degrees through an environment that offers tools for success, a sense of centrality, and sufficient numbers to eliminate issues of tokenism for African American students and faculty. Furthermore, their admissions standards "are as sensitive to the *potential* of black applicants as they are to the limits of their precollege backgrounds" (Morris, 1979, p. 201).

Summary

What are the lessons learned from the colleges dedicated to serving a particular group? As with the characteristics of successful institutions listed earlier, these institutions focus on the success of their students and presume their capacity for success. This effort is clearly facilitated by the presence of many faculty and administrators who provide role models and varieties of perspectives. Sufficient numbers enhance success and the opportunity for variety, something that is more difficult to achieve when the community contains few minorities, women, or disabled. These institutions also tend to provide whatever programmatic support is necessary as part of the educational program. All in all, a special environment—in many ways a more benign environment—exists in which individuals learn without their race or gender functioning as a stigma in their performance.

Implications: An Expanded Focus

What women's colleges can assume for women, other colleges and universities cannot assume for their students. What traditionally African American institutions can assume for African American students, others cannot assume. Yet most students do not attend these kinds of institutions, and challenges and benefits are inherent in whatever choice is made. The last 20 years have provided a myriad of opportunities for institutions to look at the issues related to diversity and to respond to them. The characteristics of successful institutions, women's colleges, and historically African American colleges and universities include programs and support services that focus on the particular needs of particular students and groups while also creating organizational climates that are positive and supportive of students' diversity. A number of handbooks and program descriptions available in the literature describe some of the successful institutional approaches to meeting a variety of students' needs (Clewell and Ficklen, 1986; Richardson, Simmons, and de los Santos, 1987; WICHE, 1987). While some, such as ACE's *Minorities on Campus* (Green, 1989), address programs for minority students and others, such as *Educating the Majority* (Pearson, Shavlik, and Touchton, 1989), address women's concerns, the themes are sufficiently consistent to be of critical importance for all institutions. The dominant focus in many of these approaches is still on the needs of the particular student group and appropriate institutional responses to those needs. This monograph began by noting how important the phrasing of questions is in shaping the answers that follow. Here again this issue must be addressed. The basic conceptual framework for many of the more traditional responses to diversity has focused on *student assistance*. Tutorial services, financial aid, ramps and braille maps, and academic support programs all reflect an effort to respond to problems that students bring with them. Fundamentally, it is a "deficit" approach to diversity in that it attempts to improve success by providing the student with support and resources. In many institutions, response has been broadened considerably through efforts to address the climate of the institution for these students. Campuses have added ethnic studies programs, ethnic support centers, women's studies programs, evening classes, and other institutional changes. These efforts to provide *institutional accommodation* still focus on the "special needs" of nontraditional students but acknowledge ways in which the institution can present barriers to success.

More and more, however, what appears throughout the literatures on the many groups that have been relegated to the margin is a set of themes requiring a shift in the ways we approach the challenge of diversity and the focus of the issue. By asking *how* an institution begins to educate and create a climate that is involving for all its members, the question is focused on fundamental aspects of the institution and its ability to embrace diversity, rather than on its ability to simply add programs or make modest changes. Recognition is increasing that specific programmatic and policy responses by themselves are not sufficient to make major strides and that more fundamental organizational shifts are required. Without this shift, all other approaches (while still important and essential) run the risk of simply helping students "adjust," "manage," or "survive" in an alien environment. "Unfortunately, many critics have been so impressed by the newly erected monuments to equal opportunity that they have failed to recognize that the foundations are the same as those [that] have for centuries perpetuated a structure of inequality of opportunity" (Morris, 1979, p. 273). A similar theme is voiced on the education of women: "Now is the time for our institutions of higher education to reshape organizational structures, question institutional values, reexamine policies and procedures, and develop plans to sincerely meet the needs of women, faculty, administrators, staff, and students" (Pearson, Shavlik, and Touchton, 1989, p. 8). The need is present to build on and maintain the efforts of those successful institutions that focus on individuals' and groups' needs and at the same time to focus on all students, all faculty, and the institution's capacity to *organize for diversity.*

Organizing for Diversity: Fundamental Issues

HIGHER EDUCATION is faced today with the necessity—and the opportunity—to once again rethink what it does and how it does it. At the core of this effort is the organization's improved capacity to educate in a pluralistic society for a pluralistic world. But to do so requires a shift in our thinking from a focus on the issues surrounding students and "the problems" they create for the institution. In addition to whether students are prepared for learning is a serious question as to whether institutions are prepared for diversity. Such a shift requires a different rationale for thinking about change. If the institution is concerned about the capacity to deal with diversity, then the attention is on the entire community. Diversity among faculty, staff, and students is seen as important not only for the support such individuals provide for specific groups but also for the importance of diverse perspectives to institutional success and quality. The institution recognizes that remediation is an issue for many students and that concern for effective teaching and learning must be a paramount objective throughout the institution. Readiness to deal with diversity requires asking about the attitudes and information of traditional students as well as nontraditional students. Indeed, at a number of institutions, programs have been developed that focus on multicultural awareness for all students through workshops and course credit. Such programs assume that individuals need education about and awareness of pluralism. The message is that educating for diversity is important for everyone to create a suitable environment for diversity, both in the university and in society (Banks, 1981; Barbarin, 1981).

On many campuses across the country, the challenges of creating an organization that embraces diversity so that it can truly begin to educate all students has begun.

Institutional self-reflection, let alone transformation, is not an easy process. It raises questions about the institution and its assumptions about the academic enterprise. Moreover, the picture of what colleges and universities should look like is not yet clear, though the research on successful institutions suggests some of the issues that institutions must address. Higher education is a highly complex, decentralized system, and within that system is an enormous array of institutions. Thus, the process of change and the specific goals for change will necessarily be specific to the institution. Nevertheless, the existing review of the literature suggests that colleges and universities—large and small, commuter and residential, public and private, urban and rural—will be asked to confront a number of challenges as diversity is addressed.

Diversification of Faculty and Staff

The call for a more diversified faculty and staff in the literature is viewed almost universally as important. The literature is clear about the importance of faculty support in general and the importance of this role in particular for nontraditional students, whether adult learners, disabled students, or minority students. Certainly an important aspect of the success of historically African American colleges and women's colleges rests on the important role of African American faculty and staff and women faculty and staff in running the institution. The emphasis on a diverse faculty and staff is indeed critical but for more reasons than are often articulated.

Five reasons emerge. The first three deal with faculty and staff roles relating to students. The most common reason given for the need to diversify faculty and staff is to provide support for the benefit of students from particular groups. Observers generally acknowledge that students in the minority will seek out a faculty member who, they perceive, understands their experience. Often this selection is based on gender, racial or ethnic commonality, or disability. Given the environment on many campuses, such faculty and staff play a very important role. Indeed, evidence suggests that such faculty and staff, because of their relatively small numbers, are often burdened by the advising and counseling that accompany their role as a member of a visible minority.

A second reason for encouraging the diversification of faculty and staff is that diversification is an important symbol to students from these groups about their own futures and about the institution's commitment to them.

Third, diversification of the campus community creates a more comfortable environment for students as well as for faculty and staff. The strains suffered by students also exist for faculty and staff members who represent diverse groups. These individuals assume the burden of being spokespersons, mentors, support persons, and symbols, while also trying to perform to rigorous professional standards. At the same time, they may endure the same kind of loneliness and insensitivities also experienced by students (Blackwell, 1988; Olivas, 1988; Smith, 1980).

The last two reasons for the importance of a diversified faculty and staff relate to benefits to the institution. Diversification of the faculty and staff is likely to contribute to what is taught, how it is taught, and what is important to learn, contributions that are vital to the institution. Faculty trained in traditional pedagogy and in traditional methodologies often find it difficult to fundamentally change courses and curricula. Diversification of the faculty and staff make it easier, because the likelihood is greater for the introduction of different perspectives and approaches and for many more opportunities for professional collaboration. People such as administrators and faculty in decision-making positions who have had their own experiences with aspects of institutional life that create barriers or even alienate students offer the institution an invaluable service by providing their perspectives on potential problem areas. It should be remembered, however, that no single individual can represent any more than his or her own perspective or be sensitive to all the issues, needs, and concerns of each disparate group that has been described. An African American faculty member, for example, cannot reflect all the issues of a disabled or a Latino student. Thus, what is needed is true diversity. Fifth, a diverse faculty and staff reflect one measure of institutional success for an educational institution in a pluralistic society. As long as the leadership of our institutions contains only token representation of persons from diverse backgrounds, institutions will not be able to claim that the goals for society or our educational institutions have been achieved.

Thus, the issue of diversity in faculty and staff assumes direct as well as indirect importance for campus efforts. While these efforts are important for students from those groups, they are also important for the institution. Concern is great, however, that being able to achieve this goal in the near future is highly unlikely (Blackwell, 1988; Sudarkasa, 1987; Valverde, 1988; Wilson, 1987a). The lack of growth in higher education over this past decade and the increased use of part-time faculty have combined to produce fewer opportunities for faculty and staff advancement. Now, projections for openings in the next decade are more optimistic, but it is almost universally recognized that the lack of retention and the lack of attractiveness in pursuing advanced degrees for today's and yesterday's undergraduates threaten institutional goals for increasing the hiring of more women and minorities (Blackwell, 1988). If the presence of a truly diversified faculty and staff is critical, this situation jeopardizes institutional efforts.

It is important to note that the barrier to diversification is not simply an issue of numbers. Availability of individuals to assume these positions is clearly a problem. Evidence suggests, however, that institutions are also having difficulty retaining faculty and staff of different backgrounds for the same reasons they have had problems retaining students. The current revolving-door pattern is an extravagant waste of human resources and a major obstacle to change. Efforts to retain and develop staff and graduate students already within the institution are therefore as important as increasing the pool of applicants to the institution.

Mission and Values

As indicated earlier, some of the values rooted in the academic tradition are now coming into question. Issues of values are not easily identified, discussed, or dealt with. Given the literature on organizational effectiveness, however, it is probably very important to identify those values that are central to the institution's mission and those that are not. It is also critical that this discussion be held in such a way that traditional assumptions may be open to question. Two sets of values are frequently cited as important: competition/cooperation and individualism/concern for community. The increasing evidence on the effectiveness of cooperative learning, for example, suggests that traditional structures that encourage competitiveness may be counterproductive to the institution and to all students (Astin, 1987; Palmer, 1987). Rather than being viewed as a threat to institutional quality, such changes may well turn out to improve institutional effectiveness. Discussions about individualism and community touch not only on matters of importance to a number of ethnic and racial groups but also on the increasing concern about narcissism and unethical behavior in society (Harris, Silverstein. and Andrews, 1989; McIntosh, 1989; Minnich, 1989). Have we gone too far in encouraging competitive and highly individualistic practices at the expense of concern for the community and at the expense of good learning?

Questions about values emerge at all levels of the institution. Perhaps one of the most challenging has to do with the ways in which students perceive that the values and perspectives they bring with them to the academic community are not appreciated and may even put them into conflict with institutional norms and behaviors. At its worst, students may perceive that they must abandon the values of their own cultures or background to succeed (Ogbu, 1978). The resulting phenomenon of alienation is contradictory to the central role being given to the importance of involvement in one's education and with the institution.

The question of values also extends to how the campus functions and to the norms and expectations for performance. As has been suggested in this monograph, grading practices, decision making, approaches to learning, residence hall lifestyles, dress, and interpersonal manners are very much affected by values and by background. Creating a campus environment in which one is free to discuss these issues and in which one can create alternative practices can be difficult. The overall pattern of teaching practices in higher education, for example, has never adequately reflected what we know about learning. Large lecture classes, lack of immediate feedback, multiple choice tests, and so on do not reflect the necessary variety in pedagogy for adequate learning (Smith, 1983). One might conjecture that as long as students could succeed despite this kind of teaching and as long as one did not care about those who did not succeed, we did not need to connect teaching with learning. Now those conditions must change. Fewer and fewer students succeed. To connect teaching with learning requires knowing about students, knowing about the subject matter, and knowing about conducive environments for learning. Perhaps because of their marginal status, more of these issues are being raised today as they relate to nontraditional students. Just one example of alternative forms of pedagogy is described in *Women's Ways of Knowing* (Belenky and Associates, 1986). Despite methodological issues about the study's ability to generalize about gender, the report does vividly describe a group of women's preference for "connected" learning. The authors describe connected learning as an interactive experience in which involvement facilitates learning. In this form of learning, empathy, care, and understanding are viewed as important parts of the process of making judgments. Class participation, collaborative projects, and students' contributing to one another's views would be seen as critical. In contrast, the values implicit in many traditional forms of pedagogy are isolation, cynicism, and competition.

Areas of new inquiry, however, are not always well received, particularly if they are not in the accepted tradition of one's colleagues or institution (Pearson, Shavlik, and Touchton, 1989). Many have viewed feminist scholarship and ethnic studies, for example, as peripheral to the curriculum and as subjects of nonserious inquiry. Moreover, some view such scholarship as contributing to the weakening of the curriculum (Bloom, 1987). The issues involved go to the heart of such questions as what constitutes a good education, what we mean by quality and how we evaluate it, and the appropriate methodologies in the search for truth. For faculty members interested in asking new questions in new areas, the risk can be great unless those areas are already seen as legitimate or unless they themselves have the status to alter approaches in their fields. And it can be very difficult for those who represent minorities in the decision-making process.

Institutions face a challenge in differentiating between those values and goals that facilitate learning and serve the institution's mission and those values that leave some groups on the margin. At the same time, it is important to be open to new ways of accomplishing goals. Evidence on the benefits of cooperative learning for all students, for example, suggests that traditional structures that build in competition may be counterproductive. Such environments may be detrimental to most students. Values and the clarification of assumptions about values are at the heart of the issue of diversity.

Dealing with Conflict

Even the most superficial analysis of what is happening on many college campuses suggests that conflict is either openly present or just under the surface. Some degree of conflict would be expected when individuals and groups from diverse backgrounds try to come together in an institutional setting (Jones, 1987). While increased numbers may be more comfortable to a member of a minority group, they may be more threatening to a member of the majority. Thus, conflict may be intensified on many campuses as they become more diverse or more explicit in their efforts to diversify. A look at the literature on intergroup relations suggests moreover that the conditions are present for conflict, given the competitive environment, unequal status of individuals and groups, frustration caused by hostile environments, and perceptions of unresponsiveness by some and favoritism by others and given that little exists to bring groups together in meaningful contact (Amir, 1969; Gamson, Peterson, and Blackburn, 1980). Building on the literature of cultural pluralism, we can expect conflict when desirable values are incompatible. Campuses, for example, are struggling with having to choose between setting desirable standards for speech and behavior and supporting rights of free speech given in the First Amendment *(Stanford Observer,* 1989). Yet the existence of conflict may be a good sign that the institution is grappling with many of these issues and is in the process of fundamental change. Indeed, a very significant study of the patterns of adaptation that occur in institutions dealing with issues of diversity suggests that conflict may be part of the process that will assist institutions to identify essential changes (Skinner and Richardson, 1988). Conflict can therefore be a pathway to learning (Green, 1989).

Though higher education is rooted in a tradition of debate and the free exchange of ideas, it is not clear that dealing with conflict, particularly the kind of conflict apt to become emotional, is one that institutions can deal with very effectively. The conflicts that can emerge from trying to create truly pluralistic environments are uncomfortable and may need to be so. The challenge is to create vehicles for dealing with conflict in an environment that is open to differences. Indeed, a characteristic of many successful campuses has been the creation of strong policies, procedures, and even special programs of mediation and arbitration to recognize the existence of conflict and to use it as a vehicle for learning by the institution (Green, 1989).

The Quality of Interaction on Campus

The body of research cited that reflects the importance of students' involvement with the institution requires an institutional assessment about involvement, how students can become involved, the level of interaction among students and between students and faculty, and the general climate of the campus for involvement. The literature on intergroup relations that suggests the need for students and faculty to participate together in meaningful and important work also supports the involvement. While residential campuses and smaller institutions have more natural potential to develop involvement, the challenge is present for all institutions. Many campuses use mentor programs, programmatic efforts at the college and departmental levels within the university, residence halls, and athletic programs to build communities of involved students and faculty. For large public institutions, the challenging question is whether meaningful learning communities can be developed that benefit from diversity.

Educating for Diversity

As institutions begin to evaluate the quality of climate for diversity, one inevitable discussion centers around the role of the educational process and in particular the role of the curriculum (Slaughter, 1988). Many more institutions are beginning to articulate a commitment to educate students for living in a pluralistic world and to create environments that embrace diversity. The content of the curriculum insofar as it serves these goals, the styles of teaching, and the modes of assessment are all being evaluated. Schools like Stanford and the University of California-Berkeley have now moved to require that all students develop some familiarity with the diversity of American cultures and with issues of race, class, and gender. Curricular transformation involves the same kind of developmental process as institutional transformation in moving from courses that address the voids in the curriculum to efforts to ask new questions that more naturally embrace the pluralism of perspectives in the field (McIntosh, 1989).

The role of pedagogy is very important to this aspect of education. Recognizing that groups and individuals may learn in different ways requires rethinking the ways in which teaching occurs. The increasing community of students with learning disabilities has focused attention on this issue, but the discussion touches on the literature concerning the adult learner, racial and ethnic groups, and women as well. In other words, it touches on more than a majority of all students.

The issue of assessment is another component of this educational challenge. Not only are the goals for assessment ambiguous in terms of the kinds of learning being evaluated; significant questions also exist about many of the forms of assessment now in place. For example, for those with learning disabilities, multiple choice, time-limited tests may be invalid indicators of learning. The controversy concerning the role of standardized tests for women and minorities reflects similar concerns about the validity of present testing approaches. Without valid indicators of learning, underestimating the performance of many populations of students is a significant risk. This controversy is being highlighted by court challenges to the means of awarding New York State scholarships to women and by criticisms of the national movement to require examinations for teachers (Duran, 1986; National Center, 1989).

The Perceived Conflict Between Access and Quality

The continuing message that a fundamental conflict exists between issues of access to the institution and quality is perhaps the most disturbing indication that present institutional approaches to diversity are inadequate (Adolphus, 1984; Birnbaum, 1988; Mingle, 1987; Rendon and Nora, 1987; Skinner and Richardson, 1988; Stewart, 1988). Given the number of national studies concerned about the effectiveness and quality of higher education and the call for increasing standards, the higher education community needs to carefully and thoughtfully address this apparent conflict.

Much of the discussion about improving institutional quality focuses on perceptions about the quality of the students being admitted and concern about lowering standards, although these perceptions can also be found in discussions about hiring and retaining faculty and staff (Gamson, 1978;

Mingle, 1987; Peterson and Associates, 1978; Willie and McCord, 1972). There is reason to believe that the questions being asked and the assumptions being made result in an inappropriate conflict between these two central values. Several important points must be made:

The concern about the preparation of students, while affecting many minority students, is not a minority problem. While the impact of poor preparation on those who come from disadvantaged backgrounds is more devastating, declining preparation of students is a national issue affecting virtually all schools and all students. Indeed, most poorly prepared students are white (SHEEO, 1987).

The concern that the admission of many minority groups represents a lowering of test scores ignores the fact that the goals of higher education with regard to admissions have always reflected different levels of preparation among its students. Even the most highly selective institutions have sought diversity in geography, artistic and athletic talent, and leadership among its students rather than populations of perfect GPAs and SATs. With these types of diversity, quality was discussed hardly at all because the educational community and the public understood that quality presumably embraced the contributions of those with different strengths. Moreover, it was widely recognized that grades and test scores could not define all that was needed for success in academics and the community. The value of diversity when it comes to students that differ markedly from the majority seems to be recognized far less, however.

Much of the evidence concerning the tension between quality and diversity rests on lower standardized scores. As indicated elsewhere, serious questions exist about the predictive validity and the power of these instruments for women, for many minorities, and for those with learning disabilities (Duran, 1986; Grubb, 1986; Morris, 1979; National Center, 1989; Sedlacek, 1986; Thomas, 1981; Wilson, 1980). The same could be said for learning assessment programs that rely on these kinds of measures. Changing measures of assessment does not mean lowering standards for learning. Indeed, one characteristic of institutions described earlier as successful is that they set high standards and expectations. We are challenged to develop adequate assessment programs and to avoid relying on inadequate programs that, because of expediency, have the effect of diminishing the evidence of performance for particular groups. Though assessment takes a different form for faculty and staff, concern exists that many institutions do not know how to evaluate the quality of scholarship or performance of those from different faculty groups as well.

The problem about quality also involves how we define success in school and a student's capacity to learn. If we assume that only one way to learn is correct and at the same time place individuals in environments that are only marginally dedicated to their success, we are setting up whole groups of students for failure. Early evidence focused attention on academic preparation as the most significant factor in achievement, leading many researchers to conclude that academic success is a function of preparation, not race (Richardson and Bender, 1987). As this monograph has suggested, however, to the degree that issues of racism, sexism, homophobia, and the general presence of an alienating environment also affect performance, then lack of performance cannot be focused entirely on the student. All too often we have assumed the institution's perfection and students' incompetence.

Care must be exercised in how we teach, about the environment in which teaching takes place, and about how we assess learning.

Numerous references in the literature suggest that the fundamental predisposition of higher education has been to maintain homogeneity and to adapt only when necessary (Morris, 1979; Verdugo, 1986). A critical example of it may be occurring now in the discussions about whether some institutions have set limits on access for Asian American students because they are "overrepresented" in the student body. The credibility of higher education's commitment to quality and diversity is weakened when access of Asian Americans is limited in the name of diversity and access of African American and Latino students is limited in the name of quality. The net result of both is to perpetuate homogeneity.

If these two concepts—diversity and quality—remain in conflict, the challenge of diversity will not be met. The questions once again are whether the conflict is real and whether we are asking the right questions. When quality is measured in one way only, conflict between quality and diversity is created

(Madrid, 1988). The implications are that we can broaden our understanding about quality without diluting expectations for learning or for the curriculum. The institution will need to carefully evaluate its standards, its performance criteria, and the climate in which learning occurs, however.

The Changing Climate

At the same time that institutions that genuinely wish to change face significant challenges, other forces facilitate a recognition of the need for change. As troubling as some of the incidents of racial harassment and sexual harassment have been, they have served to bring to the forefront the nature and depth of some of the problems within the community of higher education. Some institutions have begun to study themselves, listening to the experiences of their staff, students, and faculty while acknowledging the need for change. Many institutions, including some of the more prestigious ones, are now leading the way in their efforts to address some of these issues. At the same time, awareness is growing at the national level that major public policy and social implications are involved. Some of the recent national commissions on the achievements of minorities have been both urgent and eloquent in their calls for change and action.

Changing student demographics and the increased voice that students and staff can find in influencing institutional policy have facilitated the awareness of a need for change. It has combined with continuing institutional concern for enrollments to put students in a more influential position than they have been in during other times. This is now a time of increasing student activism. Over the next decade as large numbers of faculty retire and larger numbers of students enter the collegiate generation, we can anticipate a shift in institutional priorities from a concern for enrollment to a concern about hiring faculty, and it may well shift the focus away from the quality of students' experience to the quality of the faculty's experience (Bowen and Schuster, 1986; Smith, 1988). The improved environment for faculty, their salaries, and their hiring may assist in attracting more minorities and women to faculty positions. Some evidence suggests, for example, that it may already be occurring. While the overall numbers of minority Ph.D.s has declined in recent years, the number has actually increased for minority women (Coyle and Bae, 1987).

An organizational approach to diversity has significance for virtually all institutions regardless of the diversity within their student bodies, for it acknowledges the importance of diversity for society and for its future. The reality of demographic shifts is such that Hawaii's "minority" student enrollment is 66.4 percent and Maine's is 3.8 percent. The approach to educating for all forms of diversity—minorities, women, disabled, adult learners, and part-time learners—and the importance of educating all students to live in a pluralistic world are as relevant to Maine as they are for Hawaii, however.

By creating an organization that can deal with diversity and by taking a comprehensive approach to diversity, institutions will find themselves less fragmented in dealing with the numbers of groups with special needs. It will then be more likely that the special needs and perspectives of any number of groups will be more easily accommodated. Moreover, an institution that organizes for diversity will derive many benefits from this approach, not the least of which is the increased capacity to respond to change (Weick, 1979). Other opportunities are present as well:

- Revitalizing the curriculum;
- Developing new approaches to policy and organization;
- Modeling the development and growth of "global villages";
- Increasing dialogue and thus success concerning the characteristics of the environment that foster good teaching and learning;
- Creating an environment that appreciates the ways in which difference contributes to education;
- Clarifying the values that are essential to the academic mission and to the creation of community;
- Benefiting from the diversity of teaching approaches;
- For students, particularly but not only in residential institutions, experiencing the excitement and opportunities to learn from diversity.

In other words, opportunity is greater for much enhanced institutional success and quality.

Assessment and Implications

WHILE THE CHALLENGE of diversity is indeed a national challenge, no clearly marked paths are present to creating educational organizations prepared for this process, given the complexities involved in the concept itself and in human and organizational behavior in general. Nevertheless, consistencies emerge from a wide-ranging set of literatures suggesting some of the steps needed.

Institutional Assessment

Information is an important element in efforts to create change and to assess the need for change. One of the important initial strategies that can be applied in an institution is an assessment in which all aspects of the college or university are evaluated and can serve as a point of reference. A fundamental question frames the assessment: How is the institution doing with respect to diversity?

Because the effectiveness of research is critically related to its design, an institutional audit needs to be sure:

- That generalizations across groups are not made until the validity of such groups is confirmed;
- That the perspectives of a diverse set of constituencies and groups are involved in the design and interpretation of the results;
- That the instruments used to collect data, whether surveys, interviews, or tests, are checked for their validity and appropriateness for the campus and its constituencies and that, where possible, multiple methods are used;

- That the aspects of campus life and individual and group characteristics studied are inclusive enough to tap a broad range of issues.

Appendix A lists some of the questions that can be asked in assessing an institution's status with regard to creating an involving environment. It is by no means complete but might provide the basis for an audit guide. *Minorities on Campus* (Green, 1989) provides additional questions to broaden the focus.

Research

The need for continued research on diversity in higher education is great. Efforts to identify successful programs that may serve as models for other institutions are very important. The use of national data bases, not only to track students but also to identify institutional characteristics that facilitate success, provides important perspectives. Studies addressing institutional characteristics, however, must move beyond measures of selectivity and resources to ensure that a broader range of institutional qualities is addressed. We also need to know more about the varieties of ways in which students can be involved and how, if at all, those ways differ among specific populations. A parallel need exists, however, to track the presence and retention of faculty and staff and to look at the institutional experiences of those individuals, not only at the professional level but also at the graduate level. The Council of Graduate Schools (1986) has called for such efforts because of the centrality of faculty and staff for the efforts being considered.

A profound need also exists for greater dialogue concerning the results of empirical studies and for synthesis of results that address both theoretical and applied questions. Part of this dialogue could entail efforts to clarify apparent contradictions so that accurate conclusions can be drawn or so that further research could be developed to clarify these differences. The array of studies available that address similar questions with different methodologies and analyses and all too often reach different conclusions limits the role of the scholar and the researcher in contributing to what is actually occurring in our institutions. The loss is significant not only for educational research but also for effective institutional change.

Because institutions vary in their mission, size, complexity, and makeup, the need continues for institutional research on a number of topics that will allow individual institutions to assess their own success in educating students from widely diverse backgrounds as well as the climate of the institution for these students, for faculty and staff, and for more traditional students. Institutional research on who comes, who stays, students' satisfaction, factors associated with retention and graduation, and alumni perceptions can be very helpful in identifying issues and in creating a climate for change (Smith, 1982). Great care must be exercised in framing questions for research, however, so that "deficit" models are not reintroduced.

Coordination Among Sectors

Some of the data on educational preparation continue to reinforce the importance of quality preparation in kindergarten through grade 12 to students, to higher education, and to society as a whole. Traditionally, higher education has not directly addressed these issues except through schools of education. This review reinforces the degree of self-interest that higher education should have in issues of precollegiate education. Clearly, higher education cannot address all these issues on its own, but it is responsible for training the teachers and educators who run schools and has an important role in the nature of school systems and in the importance given to the educational profession. Higher education also produces the scholars for future generations of faculty. Moreover, the standards set for entrance and for assessment have an impact throughout the school years. The presidents of Stanford and Harvard are two leading educators who have acknowledged the importance of the role higher education should take in this effort. The nature of the education all students receive concerning issues of diversity can have a major impact throughout the educational system.

Additionally, in states where community colleges assume a significant role in the education of students—and in particular, minority and adult students—articulation between two-year and four-year institutions must be strengthened. This priority is addressed in California, which is actively attempting to address this issue through the development of a revised master plan for higher education in the state (Joint Committee, 1988). Following up on students' progress, early intervention, articulation of courses, and coordinated student services are all important features of this effort (Cohen, 1988; Donovan, Schaier-Peleg, and Forer, 1987; Richardson and Bender, 1987). Gathering data is a critical element, though trying to assess the retention and transfer rates from two-year institutions to four-year institutions is a challenge, given the diverse reasons students have for attending community colleges.

State higher education executive officers have developed an important report outlining the particularly significant role that states can play in setting policies and expectations to facilitate institutional and cooperative responses. In addition to financial support, programmatic support, and policy, states have important roles in the design and implementation of effective programs to gather data (Callan, 1988; SHEEO, 1987).

National Issues

In addition to the national studies that clarify, study, and bring attention to the challenges of diversity, a need exists for support in encouraging students to enter teaching and those fields where women and minorities have traditionally been underrepresented. Sufficient evidence suggests that previous national, corporate, and foundation efforts to encourage students to enter graduate and professional schools have been successful. That need is emerging once again as higher education prepares for a new wave of challenges and opportunities presented through the attrition of faculty hired during the growth of the sixties (Council of Graduate Schools, 1986). Related to these kinds of programs is the need to focus once again on financial assistance so that students can more reasonably choose programs appropriate to their goals. They can involve direct assistance as well as programs that forgive loan obligations for students going into certain fields, such as teaching.

Costs and Commitment

Some students are very much affected by issues of cost. Yet federal and state funding of financial aid has decreased during the last 10 years, and many institutions have seen the percentage of their resources allocated to financial aid growing larger and faster than any other portion of the budget (Stampen and Fenske, 1988). The pressures on institutional budgets and national pressure to limit the increase in growth for the costs of higher education place significant strain on institutions to limit spending. To the degree that some of the changes needed, such as increased financial aid to minority students or part-time students, add to costs, the changes will be slowed.

Perhaps one of the greatest challenges presented is the need for sustained commitment and effort. The need for change is urgent, but institutional change will not be easy or quick. With equal parts of dismay and cynicism, numbers of writers observe that higher education's concerns for such issues run in cycles. Indeed, "unless we recognize the systemic nature of persistent racial inequalities, progress . . . may never be more than marginal and episodic" (Morris, 1979, p. 269). Others suggest that it is only in response to a crisis that institutions or those involved in public policy will respond. The implication is that when the crisis ends, the commitment also ends (Adolphus, 1984). While many are calling it a crisis, the nature of the change needed will no doubt require sustained commitment. "What is needed is a level of commitment such that the risk of retreat is forever banished" (SHEEO, 1987, p. 12).

Leadership

While some authors are inclined to debate the importance of leadership in creating change, studies to date reflect the importance of institutional leadership in creating a climate for change and in achieving change. Leadership is required not only to set explicit goals and provide the resources for change but also to frame relevant questions and set the tone for the resulting discussions. For example, the dichotomy between quality and diversity needs to be eliminated so that the necessary discussions can occur in a climate that does not assume that being different is synonymous with being inferior. Energetic leadership will be required to achieve the diversity in faculty and staff that is essential to success.

Throughout the literature is the implication that some of the prevailing attitudes and values in higher education not only create a chilly climate but also may actually impede learning for many more than a minority of students. Indeed, it impedes learning for the majority. Addressing issues of cooperation versus competition and individualism versus community may result in a far healthier community and a far stronger educational system. These issues, however, require careful analysis and discussion. Sensitive and educated leadership will be required.

Conclusion

Twenty years ago a concerted effort was begun to change the shape of American higher education. In that it resulted in changes in the programs and curricula of the academy and in the makeup of its students, faculties, and staffs, these efforts have been successful. If the perspective of several decades can provide a single prevailing lesson from such changes, however, it is that to simply "add and stir" is not enough. Whether or not the melting pot will be the metaphor for pluralism, embracing diversity in all its obvious and subtle forms will be its necessary ingredient. Nearly 400 years ago, the poet John Donne observed that the loss of one person represents more than the loss of one small piece of humanity; it represents a loss to all of humanity. Donne's ancient bell tolls still, for clearly the issues of diversity have significance beyond those of the disenfranchised, beyond communities that exclude rather than include. If higher education is to meet the needs of all of its constituents, these issues must be confronted—not just because they are important to a special group but because they are vital to all institutions and the nation.

Appendix: Institutional Characteristics

Makeup of the Student Body

What is the demographic makeup of the student body at both the undergraduate and graduate levels in terms of racial and ethnic minorities, gender, age, part-time or full-time status, students with disabilities? What issues of preparation are evident in the student body? What is the retention rate of each subpopulation in relation to the whole and to each other? How do graduation rates compare? What information is available about the factors associated with success? What is changing and how are these changes viewed from the perspective of the various campus constituencies? In what ways does the institution involve students? Does the leadership among students reflect the diversity on campus?

Makeup of the Faculty and Staff

What level of diversity is present within the faculty and staff? Do significant gaps exist between the character of the student body and the character of the faculty and administration? Is it clear that standards for recruitment and promotion are fair and can be evaluated appropriately? Are faculty and staff who represent nontraditional groups concentrated in special programs or are they well represented throughout the institution? How successful is the institution in retaining and promoting such faculty and staff? What are the levels of satisfaction for the faculty and staff as a whole? For various subgroups? Does the leadership of the organization exhibit diversity?

The Physical and Visual Environment

What, if any, physical barriers exist? To what degree do the architecture, use of space, and art communicate a value of diversity?

Special Programs

Have the special needs of specific groups been audited? What is needed for whom? How successful have institutional programmatic efforts been? Are sufficient resources available to provide necessary support to students so they can succeed? What role does financial aid play in students' retention and performance? Are financial aid policies flexible enough to meet the needs of diverse student groups?

Psychosocial Environment

What are the expectations for success in the environment? What is the level of faculty, administrative, and board support for individuals and for programs? What are the attitudes within the campus community about different groups and about diversity? Is the population comfortable with differences? Do any explicit or implicit values alienate rather than involve particular groups? What are the ways in which the institution involves or fails to involve all members of the community in the institution? What are the levels of satisfaction among diverse faculty, student, staff, and board groups? What are the patterns of interaction among students and between students and faculty? What feedback do alumni have about their experiences in the institution?

The Curriculum

To what degree are students aware of the diversity in their institution and in the country? How knowledgeable are they about that diversity and about the cultures, histories, and situations of those from whom they differ? To what degree does the curriculum reflect the variety of new scholarship relating to diversity? (In some institutions, the curriculum will never be comprehensive, but being carefully selective can reflect a knowledge of and respect for diversity.) What are the educational goals for all students? What evidence exists that the institution is successful in educating for diversity? How does the institution accommodate a variety of learning styles? Are any particular values required for success? What means of assessment are currently used or considered? What barriers exist to success for each student?

Administrative Practices

Have policies been carefully scrutinized and enforced for their efforts to include, not exclude? Are inappropriate behaviors dealt with decisively? To what degree does the organizational structure involve members of diverse constituencies? Have tangible and visible efforts been made to ensure that decision making at all levels and in all areas reflects the diversity in the community? How successful have recruitment and retention of faculty and staff been? Does a program exist to encourage the professional development of faculty and staff at all levels? Does an ongoing program of research exist to assess the institution's effectiveness and success in responding to diversity? What means are available to resolve differences among campus groups and to deal with conflict as a community?

Leadership

Do visible and tangible signs of leadership focus on organizational responses to diversity? How is the presence of diversity perceived—as a contribution to the scholarly community or as a detraction? Are faculty rewarded for their successes in educating a wide range of students? Do those in leadership positions within the institution, students, faculty, staff, and board bring diverse perspectives to their roles?

References

Adolphus, S. (Ed.). (1984). *Equality postponed*. New York: CEEB.

Allen, W. (1982). Undergraduate survey of black undergraduate students attending predominantly white, state-supported universities. ED 252 615. 19 pp. MF-01; PC-01.

Allen, W. (1986). Gender and campus race differences in black student academic performance, racial attitudes, and college satisfaction. Atlanta: Southern Education Foundation. ED 268 855.

Allen, W. (1987). Black colleges vs. white colleges. *Change 19*(3), 28.

Allen, W. (1988a). The education of black students on white college campuses: What quality the experience. In M. Nettles (Ed.), *Toward black student equality in American higher education*. New York: Greenwood Press.

Allen, W. (1988b). Improving black student access and achievement in higher education. *Review of Higher Education, 11*(4), 403–416.

Allen, W., Gurin, G., and Peterson, M. W. (May 1988). Black students in white institutions: The effectiveness of different institutional responses. Unpublished proposal. Ann Arbor: University of Michigan, Center for the Study of Higher Education, Center for Afro-American Studies.

Allport, G. (1954). *The nature of prejudice*. Cambridge, MA: Addison-Wesley.

Amir, Y. (1969). Contact hypothesis in ethnic relations. *Psychological Bulletin, 71*(5), 314–342.

Anderson, T. (1987). Black encounters of racism and elitism in white academe: A critique of the system. *Journal of Black Studies, 18*(3), 259–272.

Arbeiter, S. (1987). Black enrollment. *Change, 19*(3), 14–19.

Arciniega, T. A. (1985). Hispanics and higher education: A CSU imperative. California State University, Office of the Chancellor.

Armstrong-West, S., and de la Teja, M. H. (1988). Social and psychological factors affecting the retention of minority students. In M. C. Terrell and D. J. Wright (Eds.), *From survival to success*. NASPA Monograph Series Vol. 9. HE 022 232.

Asamen, J., and Berry, G. L. (1987). Self-concept, alienation, and perceived prejudice: Implications for counseling Asian-Americans. *Journal of Multicultural Counseling and Development, 15*(4), 146–160.

Asch, A. (1984). The experience of disability: A challenge for psychology. *American Psychologist, 39,* 529–536.

Asian American Student Association. (1984). Asian American admissions at Brown University. *Integrated Education, 22*(1–3), 31–41.

Astin, A. W. (1975). *Preventing students from dropping out.* San Francisco: Jossey-Bass.

Astin, A. W. (1982). *Minorities in American higher education: Recent trends, current prospects, and recommendations.* San Francisco: Jossey-Bass.

Astin, A. W. (1984). A look at pluralism in the contemporary student population. *NASPA Journal, 21*(3), 2–11.

Astin, A. W. (1985). Involvement: The cornerstone of excellence. *Change, 17*(4), 35–39.

Astin, A. W. (1987). Competition or cooperation. *Change, 19*(5), 12–19.

Astin, A., Green, K., and Korn, W. (1987). *The American freshman: Twenty-year trends.* Los Angeles: UCLA. ED 279 279.

Astin, H. W., and Burciaga, C. P. (1981). *Chicanos in higher education: Progress and attainment.* Los Angeles: Higher Education Research Institute. ED 226 690.

Babbit, C. E., Bruback, H. J., and Thompson, M. A. (1975). Organizational alienation among black college students: A comparison of three educational settings. *Journal of College Student Personnel, 16,* 53–56.

Banks, J. A. (1981). *Education in the 80s: Multiethnic education.* Washington, DC: NEA. ED 204 192.

Barbarin, O. A. (1981). *Institutional racism and community competence.* Bethesda, MD.: NIMH. ED 222 605.

Bauer, W. K. (1981). Strategies for recruiting and retaining the nontraditional student. *College Student Personnel, 15*(3), 234–238.

Bean, J. P., and Metzner, B. S. (1985). A conceptual model of nontraditional undergraduate student attrition. *Review of Educational Research, 55*(4), 485–540.

Bechman, B. (1984). *The black student's guide to colleges.* Providence, RI: Bechman-Harris.

Beckham, B. (1988). Strangers in a strange land: The experience of blacks on white campuses. *Educational Record, 68*(4), 69(1), 74–78.

Belenky, M. F., Clinchy, B. M., Goldberger, N., and Tarule, J. M. (1986). *Women's ways of knowing.* New York: Basic Books.

Belgrave, F. Z. (1984). The effectiveness of strategies for increasing social interaction of a physically disabled person. *Journal of Applied Social Psychology, 74*(2), 147–161.

Bell-Scott, P. (1984). Black women's higher education: Our legacy. *Sage, 6*(7), 8–11.

Bennett, C., and Bean, J. (1983, April). *Explanations of attrition among black students at a predominantly white institution.* Paper presented at a meeting of the American Educational Research Association, Boston, MA.

Bennett, C., and Okinaka, A. (1984). Explanations of black student attrition in predominantly white and predominantly black universities. *Integrated Education, 22*(13), 73–80.

Bimbaum, R. (1988). Administrative commitments and minority enrollments: College presidents' goals for quality and access. *Review of Higher Education, 11*(4), 435–458.

Blackwell, J. E. (1987). *Mainstreaming outsiders.* New York: General Hall.

Blackwell, J. E. (1988). Faculty issues: The impact on minorities. *Review of Higher Education, 11*(8), 417–434.

Blake, E. (1987). Equality for blacks. *Change, 19*(3), 10–13.

Blakely, W. (1987). Take a leaf from Joe Poterno: An interview with William Blakely. *Change, 19*(3), 41–43.

Bloom, A. (1987). *The closing of the American mind.* New York: Touchton.

Bodenkoop, M. S., and Johansen, M. K. (1980). Do reentry women have special needs? *Psychology of Women Quarterly, 4*(4), 591–595.

Bornholdt, L. (1987). Time for a second generation effort. *Change, 19*(3), 6–7.

Bowen, H., and Schuster, J. (1986). *American professors: A national resource imperiled.* New York: Oxford University Press.

Bowser, B. P., and Hunt, R. G. (1981). *Impacts of racism in white Americans.* Beverly Hills, CA: Sage.

Boyd, W. M. (1982). The secret of minority retention. *AGB Reports, 24*(2), 17–21.

Boyer, E. (1986). *College: The undergraduate experience in America.* New York: Carnegie Commission for the Advancement of Teaching.

Braddock, J. H. (1978). Radicalism and alienation among black college students. *Negro Educational Review, 29*(1), 4–21.

Braddock, J., and McPartland, J. (1988). Some cost and benefit considerations for black college students attending predominantly white versus predominantly black universities. In M. Nettles, (Ed.), *Toward black undergraduate student equality in American higher education.* New York: Greenwood Press.

Brown, G. H., Rosen, N. L., and Hill, S. T. (1980). *The condition of education for Hispanic Americans.* Washington, DC: Center for Education Statistics. ED 188 853. 279 pp. MF-01; PC-12.

Brown, T. H. (1982). "Testimony to the National Commission on Excellence in Education" at a public hearing in Chicago. ED 237 016. 9 pp. MF-01; PC-01.

Bruner, J. (1983). *In search of mind: Essays in autobiography.* New York: Harper and Row.

Burgos-Sasscer, R. (1987). Empowering Hispanic students: A prerequisite is adequate data. *Journal of Educational Equity and Leadership, 7*(7), 21–36.

Burrell, L. F. (1980). Is there a future for black students on predominantly white campuses? *Integrated Education, 18*(5–6), 23–27.

California Community Colleges, Chancellor's Office. (1986). Disabled students in the California community colleges: A report. Long Beach: Author.

Callan, P. M. (1988). Minority degree achievement and the state policy environment. *Review of Higher Education, 11*(4), 355–364.

Cardoza, J. (1986). Colleges alerted: Pay attention to minorities—or risk future survival. *ETS Development, 32*(2), 8–10.

Carnegie Foundation for the Advancement of Teaching. (1987). Minority access: A question of equity. *Change, 19*(3), 35–39.

Carodo, T. J., and Mangano, J. A. (1982, March). *The making and seeding of RASP: Development and dissemination of a model to ease the reentry process of adult students in two-year colleges.* Paper presented at a meeting of the American Educational Research Association. ED 223 307. 32 pp. MF-01; PC-02.

Carter, D., Pearson, C. S., and Shavlik, D. (1988). Double jeopardy: Women of color in higher education. *Educational Record, 69*(1), 86–103.

Carter, R. T., and Sedlacek, W. E. (1984). *Interracial contact, background, and attitudes: Implications for campus programs.* Research Report No. 13–84. College Park: University of Maryland. ED 268 422. 15 pp. MF-01; PC-01.

Carter, R. T., White, T. J., and Sedlacek, W. E. (1985). *White students' attitude toward Black: Implications for recruitment and retention.* Research Report No. 12–85. College Park: University of Maryland. ED 278 330.

Carver, C. S., Glass, D. C., and Katz, I. (1978). Favorable evaluations of blacks and the handicapped: Positive prejudices, unconscious denial, or social desirability? *Journal of Applied Social Psychology, 8,* 97–106.

Castaneda, A. (1974). Ideological issues of assimilation in America. In E. G. Epps (Ed.), *Cultural pluralism.* Berkeley, CA: McCutchan.

Center for Education Statistics. (1986). *Growth in higher education enrollment: 1978 to 1985.* Washington, DC: Author. ED 284 471.

Center for Education Statistics. (1987). *Digest of education statistics.* Washington, DC: Thomas D. Snyder. ED 282 359.

Chacon, M. A., Cohen, E. G., and Strover, S. (1986). Chicanas and Chicanos: Barriers to progress. In M. A. Olivas (Ed.), *Latino college students.* New York: Teachers College Press.

Chew, C. A., and Ogi, A. Y. (1987). Asian American college student perspectives. In D. J. Wright (Ed.), *Responding to the needs of today's minority students.* New Directions for Student Services, No. 38. San Francisco: Jossey-Bass.

Clark, B. R. (1972). The organizational saga in higher education. *Administrative Science Quarterly, 17*(2), 178–184.

Claxton, C. S., and Murrell, P. H. (1987). *Learning styles: Implications for improving educational practices.* ASHE-ERIC Higher Education Report No. 4. Washington, DC: Association for the Study of Higher Education. ED 293 478.

Clewell, B., and Ficklen, M. S. (1986). *Improving minority retention in higher education: A search for effective institutional practices.* Princeton, NJ: Educational Testing Service. ED 299 841.

Clowes, D. A., Hinkle, D. E., and Smart, J. C. (1986). Enrollment patterns in postsecondary education, 1961–82. *Journal of Higher Education, 57*(2), 121–133.

Cohen, A. M. (1988). Degree achievement by minorities in community colleges. *Review of Higher Education, 11*(4), 383–402.

The college president: A new survey by the ACE. (1988, March 30). *Chronicle of Higher Education,* p. A14.

Commission on Minority Participation in Education and American Life. (1988). *One-third of a nation.* Washington, DC: American Council on Education.

Cope, R. G., and Hannah, W. (1975). *Revolving-door colleges: The causes and consequences of dropping out, stopping out, and transferring.* New York: Wiley.

Council of Graduate Schools. (1986). *CGS task force on minorities in graduate education.* ED 276 396.

Courage, R. (1984, November). *What's different about teaching adult student writers?* Paper presented at a meeting of the National Council of Teachers of English. ED 259 372. 29 pp. MF-01; PC-02.

Cox, W. E., and Jobe, C. C. (1988). Recruiting wars: Can higher education compete with the military? *Educational Record, 68*(4)-69(1), 63–69.

Coyle, S., and Bae, Y. (1987). *Summary report: 1986 doctorate recipients from U. S. universities.* Washington, DC: National Academy Press.

Creange, R. (1980). *Student support services: Reentry women need them too.* Washington, DC: Association of American Colleges. ED 196 338.

Cross, K. P., and Astin, H. (1981). Factors affecting black student persistence. In G. E. Thorns (Ed.), *Black students in higher education.* Westport, CT: Greenwood Press.

Crosson, P. H. (1988). Four-year college and university environments for minority degree achievement. *Review of Higher Education, 11*(4), 365–382.

Davis, J. E., and Nettles, M. T. (1987). *Academic profession and students at public and private historically black colleges.* Paper presented at a meeting of the Association for the Study of Higher Education. ED 281 462.

de los Santos, A. G. (1986, March). *Facing the facts about Mexican America.* Paper presented at a meeting of the American Association for Higher Education, Washington, DC. ED 271 081.

Demetrulias, D. A., Sattler, J. L., and. Graham, L. P. (1982, Summer). How do you know when you are hungry? Disabled students in university settings. *Journal of NAWDAC, 45,* 8–13.

Desjardins, C. (1989). The meaning of Gilligan's concept of 'different voice' for the learning environment. In C. S. Pearson, D. L. Shavlik, and J. Touchton (Eds.), *Educating the majority: Women challenge tradition in higher education.* New York: Macmillan.

DiCesare, A., Sedlacek, W. E., and Brooks, G. C. (1972). Nonintellectual correlates of black student attrition. *Journal of College Student Personnel, 13,* 319–324.

Dinka, F., Mazzella, F., and Pilant, D. E. (1980). Reconciliation and confirmation: Blacks and whites at a predominantly white university. *Journal of Black Studies, 7*(1), 55–76.

Dix, L. S. (Ed.). (1987). *Minorities: Their underrepresentation and career differentials in science and engineering.* Washington, DC: National Academy Press. ED 285 751.

Donovan, R. A., Schaier-Peleg, B., and Forer, B. (Eds.). (1987). *Transfer: Making it work. A community college report.* Washington, DC: American Association of Community and Junior Colleges. ED 281 579.

Duffy, Y. (1989). Enhancing the effectiveness of postsecondary education for women with disabilities. In C. S. Pearson, D. L. Savlik, and J. G. Touchton (Eds.), *Educating the majority: Women challenge tradition in higher education.* New York: Macmillan.

Duhon, R. M. (1986, February). *Meeting the needs of special populations: Off-campus minority students.* Paper presented at a meeting of the Association of Teacher Education, Atlanta, Georgia.

Duran, R. P. (1986). Prediction of Hispanics' college achievement. In M. A. Olivas (Ed.), *Latino college students*. New York: Teachers College Press.

Durnell, P. L. (1980). *A needs assessment of nontraditional women students at the University of Georgia*. Atlanta: University of Georgia. ED 195 219.

Edelman, J. M. (1977). *Political language: Words that succeed and policies that fail*. New York: Academic Press.

Elam, J. C. (1982). *Black on white campuses*. Washington, DC: National Association for Equal Opportunities in Higher Education.

El-Khawas, E. (1987). *Campus trends*. Report No. 75. Washington, DC: American Council on Education. ED 286 402.

Epps, E. G., (Ed.). (1974). *Cultural pluralism*. Berkeley, CA: McCutchan.

Estrada, L. F. (1988). Anticipating the demographic future. *Change, 20*(3), 14–19.

Etzioni, A. (1968). *The active society*. New York: Free Press.

Feldman, K. A., and Newcomb, T. M. (1969). *The impact of college on students*. San Francisco: Jossey-Bass.

Fenderson, D. A. (1984). Opportunities for psychologists in disability research. *American Psychologist, 39*, 524–528.

Fichten, C. S. (1986). Attitudes and beliefs which facilitate or hamper the integration of students with physical disabilities in postsecondary education. In H. Yuker (Ed.), *Attitudes toward persons with disabilities*. New York: Greenwood Press.

Fields, C. (1988). The Hispanic pipeline: Narrow, leaking, and needing repair. *Change, 20*(3), 20–27.

Fiske, E. B. (1988). The undergraduate Hispanic: Juggling two cultures. *Change, 20*(3), 29–33.

Fleming, J. (1984). *Blacks in college*. San Francisco: Jossey-Bass.

Fox, R. N. (1985, April). *Application of a conceptual model of college withdrawal to disadvantaged students*. Paper presented at a meeting of the American Educational Research Association, Chicago, Illinois. ED 257 339.

Frances, C. (1980, July/August). Apocalyptic vs. strategic planning. *Change, 19*–44.

Frazier, E. F. (1957). *The Negro in the United States*. New York: Macmillan.

Freedman, T. (1981). Is civility on the campus threatened? *Educational Record, 62*(3), 51–53.

Fries, J. E. (1987). *The American Indian in higher education: 1975–76 to 1984–85*. Washington, DC: Center for Education Statistics. ED 281 693.

Gamson, Z. F. (1978). Programs for black students, 1968–1974. In M. W. Peterson and Associates (Eds.), *Black students on white campuses: The impact of increased black enrollment*. Ann Arbor: Institute for Social Research, University of Michigan.

Gamson, Z., Peterson, M. W., and Blackburn, R. T. (1980). States in the response of white colleges and universities to black students. *Journal of Higher Education, 51*, 255–267.

Garza, R. T., and Nelson, D. B. (1973). A comparison of Mexican and Anglo-American student perceptions of the university environment. *Journal of College Student Personnel, 14*(5), 399–401.

Gillespie, B. (1983, April). *Financing traditionally black institutions of higher education.* Paper presented at the Blacks in Higher Education Conference, Washington, DC. ED 234 113.

Gittell, M. (1985). Reaching the hard to reach. *Change, 17*(4), 51–60.

Glennen, R. E., Boxley, D. M., and Farren, P. J. (1985). Impact of intrusive advising on minority student retention. *College Student Journal, 19*(4), 335.

Goldberg, B., and Associates (1985). *Perceived effects of a financial aid scholarship on returning women students.* Research Report No. 7–85. College Park: University of Maryland. ED 272 088.

Gordon, M. (1964). *Assimilation in American life.* New York: Oxford University Press.

Green, M. (1989). *Minorities on campus: A handbook for enhancing diversity.* Washington, DC: American Council on Education.

Griffith, A. R. (1978). A cultural perspective for counseling blacks. *Journal of College Student Personnel, 19*, 249–254.

Grubb, H. J. (1986, March). *Prediction of college academic functioning: Similarities and differences between blacks and whites.* Paper presented at a meeting of the Southeastern Psychological Association, Kissimmee, Florida.

Gurin, P., and Epps, E. G. (1975). *Black consciousness, identity, and achievement.* New York: Wiley.

Guyette, S., and Heth, C. (1983, April). *American Indian higher education: Needs and projections.* Paper presented at the annual conference of the American Educational Research Association, Montreal, Quebec, Canada. ED 232 810.

Hall, E. R. (1984). *Minority students at the University of Wisconsin-Milwaukee: Who are they and how are they doing?* Paper presented at a meeting of the Wisconsin Educational Research Association. ED 249 829.

Hall, E. R. (1986). *Role demands and college experiences of minority and white men and women.* Paper presented at an AIR Annual Forum. ED 280 387.

Hameister, B. (1984). Orienting disabled students. In M. L. Upcraft (Ed.), *Orienting students to college.* New Directions for Student Services, No. 25. San Francisco: Jossey-Bass.

Harris, J., Silverstein, J., and Andrews, D. (1989). Educating women in science. In C. S. Pearson, D. L. Shavlik, and J. G. Touchton (Eds.), *Educating the majority: Women challenge tradition in higher education.* New York: Macmillan.

Hart, P. S. (1984). *Institutional effectiveness in the production of black baccalaureates.* Southern Education Foundation. ED 246 748.

Hartnett, R. I. (1970). Differences in selected attitudes and colleges or between black students attending traditionally Negro and traditionally white institutions. *Sociology of Education, 43*(4), 419–436.

Health Resource Center. (1987). *National Clearinghouse on Postsecondary Education for Handicapped Individuals: Resource directory.* Washington, DC: American Council on Education.

Hetherington, C., and Hudson, G. (1981). Returning women students: Independence, personal identity, confidence, and goal orientation. *Journal of College Student Personnel, 22*(1), 31–36.

Hill, S. T. (1984). Participation of black students in higher education: A statistical profile. *Integrated Education, 22*(1–3), 53–59.

Hilton, T. (1986). Balanced high school program more likely to lead to advanced study. *ETS Development, 32*(1), 6.

Hodgkinson, H. (1985). *All one system: Demographics of education, kindergarten through graduate school.* Washington, DC: Institute of Educational Leadership. ED 261 101.

Hsia, J. (1987, April). *Asian American students: Ability, achievement, and access to higher education.* Paper presented at a meeting of the American Educational Research Association, Washington, DC.

Hsia, J. (1988). Asian Americans fight the myth of the super student. *Educational Record, 68*(4)-69(1), 94–97.

Hu, M. (1985). Determining the needs and attitudes of nontraditional students. *Colleges and Universities, 60*(3), 201–209.

Hughes, R. (1983). The nontraditional student in higher education: A synthesis of the literature. *NASPA Journal, 20*(3), 51–64.

Hunt, C. L. (1975). Alternate patterns of minority group adjustment in the university. *Educational Forum, 39*(2), 137–147.

Jaimes, M. A. (1980). Higher educational needs of Indian students. *Integrated Education, 9*(1–2), 7–12.

Jaramillo, M. L. (1988). Institutional responsibility in the provision of educational experiences to the Hispanic American female student. In T. McKenna and F. I. Ortiz (Eds.), *The broken web*. Encino, CA: Floricanto Press.

Jarrow, J. E. (1987). Integration of individuals with disabilities in higher education: A review of the literature. *Journal of Post-secondary Education and Disability, 5*, 38–57.

Johnson, D. W., Johnson, R. T., and Mariyama, G. (1983). Interdependence and interpersonal attraction among heterogeneous and homogeneous individuals: A theoretical formulation and a meta-analysis of the research. *Review of Educational Research, 53*(1), 5–54.

Joint Committee for Review of the Master Plan in Higher Education. (1988). California faces California's future: Education for citizenship in a multicultural society. Sacramento: Author.

Jones, C. J., Harris, L. J., and Hanch, W. E. (1975). Differences in the perceived sources of academic difficulties: Black students in predominantly black and predominantly white colleges. *Journal of Negro Education, 44*, 519–529.

Jones, W. T. (1987). Enhancing minority-white peer interactions. In D. J. Wright (Ed.), *Responding to the needs of today's minority students*. New Directions for Student Services, No. 38. San Francisco: Jossey-Bass.

Kanter, R. M. (1977). *Men and women of the corporation*. New York: Basic Books.

Katz, J. H., and Ivey, Y. A. (1977). White awareness: The frontier of racism awareness training. *Personality and Guidance Journal, 55*, 485–489.

Kirchner, C., and Simon, Z. (1984). Blind and visually handicapped college students. Part I: Estimated number. *Journal of Visual Impairment and Blindness, 78*(2), 78–81.

Knowles, M. (1978). *The adult learner: A neglected species.* Houston: Gulf Publishing.

Konrad, A. M., and Gutek, B. A. (1987). Theory and research on group composition: Applications to the status of women and ethnic minorities. In S. Oskamp and S. Spacapan (Eds.), *Interpersonal processes of the Claremont Symposium on Applied Social Psychology.* Beverly Hills, CA: Sage.

Korolewicz, M., and Korolewicz, A. (1985). Effects of sex and race on interracial dating preferences. *Psychological Reports, 57,* 291–296.

Kraiger, K., and Ford, J. K. (1985). A meta-analysis of rater race effects in performance ratings. *Journal of Applied Psychology, 70*(1), 56–65.

Krupnick, C. G. (1985, May). Women and men in the classroom: Inequality and its remedies. *On Teaching and Learning,* 18–25.

LaCounta, D. W. (1987). American Indian students in college. In D. J. Wright (Ed.), *Responding to the needs of today's minority students.* New Directions for Student Services, No. 38. San Francisco: Jossey-Bass.

Lang, M. (1987, November). *Recent trends in black student retention in higher education: A statistical synthesis.* Paper presented at a meeting of Black Student Retention in Higher Education, Tampa, Florida.

Larwood, L., Gutek, B. A., and Gattiker, U. E. (1984). Perspectives on institutional discrimination and resistance to change. *Group and Organizational Studies, 9*(3), 333–352.

Lasser, C. (Ed.). (1987). *Educating men and women together.* Carbondale: University of Illinois.

Lee, J. B., Rotermund, M. K., and Bertselman, J. A. (1985). *Student aid and minority enrollment in higher education.* Washington, DC: American Association of State Colleges and Universities.

Lee, V. (1985). *Access to higher education: The experience of Blacks, Hispanics, and low SES whites.* Washington, DC: American Council on Education. ED 258 505.

Le Flore, F. (1982). Fannie: Claiming an integrated experience—The parties are all segregated. *Journal of Education Today, 15*(4), 4–5.

Livingston, M. D., and Stewart, M. A. (1987). Minority students on a white campus: Perception is truth. *NASPA Journal, 24*(3), 40–49.

Loo, C. M., and Rolison, G. (1986). Alienation of ethnic minority students at a predominantly white university. *Journal of Higher Education, 57*(1), 59–77.

Lopez, M., and Clyde-Synder, M. (1983). Higher education for the learning-disabled students. *NASPA Journal, 20*(4), 34–39.

Lunneborg, P., and Lunneborg, C. E. (1985). Student-centered vs. university-centered problems of minority students. *Journal of College Student Personnel, 26*(3), 224–228.

Lynch, D. O. (1985). *Access, involvement, and excellence: A theoretical framework.* Paper presented at the University of Wisconsin Multicultural Conference, Milwaukee, Wisconsin. ED 273 233.

McBay, S. (1986). *The racial climate on the MIT campus.* Boston: Massachusetts Institute of Technology.

McClain, B. R. (1979). The need for black colleges: A black perspective. *Crisis, 86*(5), 151–154.

McIntosh, P. (1989). Curricular revision: The new knowledge for a new age. In C. S. Pearson, D. L. Shavlik, and J. G. Touchton (Eds.), *Educating the majority: Women challenge tradition in higher education.* New York: Macmillan.

McIntyre, J. L. (1981). *Nontraditional strategies for nontraditional students.* ED 205 899.

McKenna, T., and Ortiz, F. (Eds.). (1988). *The broken web.* Encino, CA: Floricanto Press.

Madden, M. E., Woods, S. M., Dares-Hobbs, S., and Collins, J. (1987). Perceived control and student involvement in campus activities. *Journal of College Student Personnel, 28*(4), 370–371.

Madrid, A. (1988, March). *Diversity and its discontents.* Paper presented at a national conference of the American Association for Higher Education, Washington, DC.

Madrozo-Peterson, R., and Rodriguez, M. (1978). Minority students' perceptions of a university environment. *Journal of College Student Personnel, 19,* 259–264.

Mallinckrodt, B., and Sedlacek, W. E. (1987). Student retention and the use of campus facilities by race. *NASPA Journal, 24*(3), 28–32.

Marion, P. B., and Iovacchini, E. V. (1983). Services for handicapped students in higher education: An analysis of national trends. *Journal of College Student Personnel, 24,* 131–137.

Martin, J. R. (1985). Becoming educated: A journey of alienation or integration. *Journal of Education, 167*(3), 71–84.

Martinez, A., and Sedlacek, W. E. (1983). Changes in the social climate of a campus over a decade. *College and University, 58,* 254–257.

Maryland State Board for Higher Education. (1981). *Enhancement of Maryland's predominantly black collegiate institutions.* ED 214 422. 333 pp. MF-01; PC-14.

Masland, A. T. (1985). Organizational culture in the study of higher education. *Review of Higher Education, 8*(2), 157–168.

Maynard, M. (1980). Can universities adapt to ethnic minority students' needs? *Journal of College Student Personnel, 21*(4), 398–401.

Mick, L. B. (1985). Connecting link between secondary and post-secondary programs for learning disabled persons. *Journal of College Student Personnel, 26*(5), 463–465.

Minatoya, L. Y., and Sedlacek, W. E. (1984). Assessing attitudes of white university students toward blacks in a changing context. *Journal of Nonwhite Concern in Personnel and Guidance, 12,* 69–79.

Mingle, J. R. (1987). *Focus on minorities: Trends in higher education participation and success.* Education Commission of the States/SHEEO. ED 287 404.

Minnich, E. (1989). From the circle of the elite to the world of the whole. In C. S. Pearson, D. L. Shavlik, and J. G. Touchton (Eds.), *Educating the majority: Women challenge tradition in higher education.* New York: Macmillan.

Morris, L. (1979). *Elusive equality.* Washington, DC: Howard University Press.

Morris, L. (1981). The role of testing in institutional selectivity and black access to higher education. In G. E. Thorns (Ed.), *Black students in higher education.* Westport, CT: Greenwood Press.

Myrdal, G. (1962). *An American dilemma.* New York: Harper and Row.

National Center for Fair and Open Testing. (1989). *Fair Test Examiner, 3*(1), 1–3.

Neher, W. W. (1985). *Recruitment and retention of minority students in small colleges.* ED 259 408.

Nelms, C. (1982). Minorities and the professions. *Action in Teacher Education, 4*(2), 47–52.

Nettles, M. T. (1986). Black and white students' college performance in majority white and majority black academic settings. In J. Williams (Ed.), *Title VI regulations for higher education: Problems and progress.* New York: Teachers College Press.

Nettles, M. T. (1988a). Black and white students' academic performance in majority white and majority black college settings. In J. B. Williams, III (Ed.), *Desegregating America's colleges and universities.* New York: Teachers College Press.

Nettles, M. T. (1988b). *Toward black undergraduate student equality in American higher education.* Westport, CT: Greenwood Press.

Nettles, M. T., and Johnson, J. R. (1987). Race, sex, and other factors as determinants of college students' socialization. *Journal of College Student Personnel, 28*(6), 512–524.

Nettles, M. T., Thoeny, A. R., and Gosman, E. J. (1986). Comparative and predictive analyses of black and white students' college achievement and experiences. *Journal of Higher Education, 57,* 289–318.

Nettles, M. T., Thoeny, A. R., and Gosman, E. J. (1987). Racial differences in college student achievement. In A. S. Pruitt (Ed.), *In pursuit of equality in higher education.* New York: General Hall.

Nora, A. (1987). Determinants of retention among Chicano college students: A structural model. *Research in Higher Education, 26*(1), 31–57.

Oates, M. J., and Williamson, S. (1978). Women's colleges and women achievers. *Signs: Journal of Women in Culture and Society, 3*(4), 795–806.

O'Barr, J. F. (1989). Reentry women in the academy. In C. S. Pearson, D. L. Shavlik, and J. G. Touchton (Eds.), *Educating the majority: Women challenge tradition in higher education.* New York: Macmillan.

Ogbu, J. J. (1978). *Minority education and caste: The American system in cross-cultural perspective.* New York: Academic Press.

Olivas, M. A. (1986). Research on Latino college students: A theoretical framework and inquiry. In M. A. Olivas (Ed.), *Latino college students.* New York: Teachers College Press.

Olivas, M. A. (1988). Latino faculty at the border. *Change, 20*(3), 6–9.

Oliver, J., and Etcheverry, R. (1987). Factors influencing the decisions of academically talented black students to attend college. *Journal of Negro Education, 56*(2), 152–161.

Oliver, M. L., and Associates (1985). Brown and black in white: The social adjustment and academic performance of Chicano and black students in a predominantly white university. *Urban Review, 17*(1), 3–23.

Ostar, A. W. (1985, July). Quality and education in higher education. *Higher Education and National Affairs, 34,* 7.

Pace, C. R. (1984). *Measuring the quality of college student experiences.* Los Angeles: University of California-Los Angeles, Higher Education Research Institute. ED 255 099. 142 pp. MF-01; PC-06.

Palmer, P. J. (1987). Community conflict and ways of knowing. *Change, 19*(5), 20–25.

Pantages, T. J., and Creedon, C. F. (1978). Studies of college attrition: 1950–1975. *Review of Educational Research, 48,* 49–101.

Parker, W. M., Scott, J., and Chambers, A. (1985). Creating an inviting atmosphere for college students from ethnic minority groups. *Journal of College Student Personnel, 26*(1), 82–84.

Pascarella, E. T. (1980). Student-faculty informal contact and college outcomes. *Review of Educational Research, 50,* 545–595.

Pascarella, E. T. (1985). Racial differences in factors associated with bachelor's degree completion: A nine-year followup. *Research in Higher Education, 23*(4), 351–373.

Pascarella, E. T., Smart, J. C., and Stoecker, J. (1989). Race and the early status attainment of black students. *Journal of Higher Education, 60*(1), 82–107.

Patterson, A. M., and Sedlacek, W. E. (1984). Differences among minority student backgrounds and attitudes toward a university and its services. *Integrated Education, 22*(1–3), 95–101.

Patterson, A. M., Sedlacek, W. E., and Perry, F. W. (1984). Perceptions of blacks and Hispanics of two campus environments. *Journal of College Student Personnel, 25,* 513–518.

Patterson, A. M., Sedlacek, W. E., and Scales, W. R. (1984). *The other minority: Disabled student backgrounds and attitudes toward their university and its services.* Research report No. 8–84. College Park: University of Maryland. ED 275 102.

Pearson, C. S., Shavlik, D. L., and Touchton, J. G. (Eds.). (1989). *Educating the majority: Women challenge tradition in higher education.* New York: Macmillan.

Perry, D. C. (1981). The disabled student and college counseling. *Journal of College Student Personnel, 22,* 533–538.

Perry, F., and Tucher, A. B. (1981). Organizing the institution to meet the needs of minority and disadvantaged students. *College Student Journal, 15*(2), 185–189.

Peterson, M. W., Blackburn, R. T., Garrison, R., Arce, J., Davenport, T., and Mingle, M. (1978). *Black students on white campuses.* Ann Arbor: Institute for Social Research, University of Michigan. ED 162 601.

Pettigrew, T. F. (1985). New black-white patterns: How best to conceptualize them. *Annual Review of Sociology, 11,* 329–346.

Pfeffer, J. (1983). Organizational demography. *Research in Organizational Behavior, 5,* 299–357.

Pfeffer, J. (1985). Organizational demography: Implications for management. *California Management Review, 28*(1), 67–81.

Phillips, W. N., and Blumberg, R. L. (1982, April). *Tokenism and organizational change: Theoretical examination of an aspect of race relations in educational context.* Paper presented at a meeting of the American Educational Research Association. ED 213 815.

Ponterotto, J. G., Grieger, I., and Heaphy, T. J. (1985). Students together against racial separation. *Journal of College Student Personnel, 26*(3), 251–253.

Pounds, A. W. (1987). Black students' needs on predominantly white campuses. In D. J. Wright (Ed.), *Responding to the needs of today's minority students.* New Directions for Student Services, No. 38. San Francisco: Jossey-Bass.

Quevedo-Garcia, E. L. (1987). Facilitating the development of Hispanic college students. In D. J. Wright (Ed.), *Responding to the needs of today's college students.* New Directions for Student Services, No. 38. San Francisco: Jossey-Bass.

Rasor, M. (1981). *EOP and SAA undergraduates who left.* University of California-Davis. ED 213 361.

Rendón, L., and Nora, A. (1987). *Hispanics in the educational pipeline.* Unpublished paper. Irvine: RAZA Advocates for California Higher Education.

Rendón, L., and Nora, A. (1988). Hispanic students. *Educational Record, 68*(4)-69(1), 79–85.

Rice, J. K., and Hemmings, A. (1988). Women's colleges and women achievers: An update. In E. Minnich, J. O'Barr, and R. Ronnfield (Eds.), *Reconstructing the academy: Women's education and women's studies.* Chicago: University of Chicago Press.

Richardson, R. C., Jr., and Bender, L. W. (1987). *Fostering minority access and achievement in higher education.* San Francisco: Jossey-Bass.

Richardson, R. C., Jr., and de los Santos, A. (1988). From access to achievement: Fulfilling the promise. *Review of Higher Education, 11*(4), 323–328.

Richardson, R. C., Jr., Simmons, H., and de los Santos, A. (1987). Graduating minority students. *Change, 19*(3), 20–22. Richardson, S. A. (1976). Attitudes and behavior toward the physically handicapped. *Birth defects: Original article series* 12, 15–4.

Rochin, R., and de la Tones, A. (1987). Strengthening Chicano studies programs. *La Red/The Net, 1*(1), 11–30.

Rokeach, M. (1972). *Beliefs, attitudes, and values.* San Francisco: Jossey-Bass.

Rooks, C. J. (1988, June). *How to keep ethnic diversity on the agenda.* Speech given at Career Day, Long Beach, California.

Rooney, G. D. (1985). Minority students' involvement in minority student organizations: An exploratory study. *Journal of College Student Personnel, 26*(5), 450–455.

Rossi, A. (1987). Coeducation in a grades-stratified society. In C. Lasser (Ed.), *Educating men and women together.* Carbondale: University of Illinois.

Roueche, J. E., and Baker, III, G. A. (1987). *Access and excellence.* Washington, DC: Community College Press.

Salganik, L. H., and Maw, C. E. (1987, April 20–24). *Factors affecting Hispanics' participation and persistence in postsecondary education.* Paper presented at a meeting of the American Educational Research Association, Washington, DC.

Sanders, D. (1987). Cultural conflicts: An important factor in the academic failures of American Indian students. *Journal of Multicultural Counseling and Development, 15*(2), 81–90.

Sandler, B. R. (1987). The classroom climate: still a chilly one for women. In C. Lasser (Ed.), *Educating men and women together.* Carbondale: University of Illinois.

Sandler, B., and Hall, R. M. (1982). *The classroom climate: a chilly one for women?* Washington, DC: Association of American Colleges.

Saslow, R. S. (1981). A new student for the eighties: The mature woman. *Educational Horizons, 60*(1), 41–61.

Schmidt, M. R., and Sprandel, H. Z. (1982). *Helping the learning disabled student.* New Directions for Student Services, No. 18. San Francisco: Jossey-Bass.

Sedlacek, W. E. (1982). *The validity and reliability of a noncognitive measure of nonstudent retention.* Research Report No. 3–82. College Park: University of Maryland.

Sedlacek, W. E. (1986). Sources of method bias in test bias research. In R. C. Wood and G. H. Hanford (Eds.), *Measures in the college admissions process.* New York: CEEB.

Sedlacek, W. E. (1987). *Black students on white campuses: 20 years of research.* Research report No. 5–87. College Park: University of Maryland.

Sedlacek, W. E., and Brooks, Jr., G. C. (1976). *Racism in American education: A model for change.* Chicago: Nelson-Hall.

Sedlacek, W. E., and Webster, D. W. (1978). Admission and retention of minority students in large universities. *Journal of College Student Personnel, 19,* 242–248.

Seeman, M. (1959). On the meaning of alienation. *American Sociological Review, 24*(6), 783–791.

Shavlik, D., Touchton, J., and Pearson, C. (1989). The new agenda of women for higher education. In C. S. Pearson, D. L. Shavlik, and J. G. Touchton (Eds.), *Educating the majority: women challenge tradition in higher education.* New York: Macmillan.

SHEEO (State Higher Education Executive Officers). (1987). *A difference of degrees: State initiative to improve minority student achievement.* Research report. Denver, CO: SHEEO.

Simmons, C. E. (1978). Women's colleges: A new agenda. *Educational Record, 59*(2), 176–182.

Skinner, E. F., and Richardson, Jr., R. C. (1988, November). *Resolving access/quality tensions: Minority participation and achievement in higher education.* Paper presented at a meeting of the Association for the Study of Higher Education, St. Louis, Missouri. HE 022 096.

Slaughter, J. B. (1988). From isolation to mainstream: An institutional commitment. In M. C. Terrell and D. J. Wright (Eds.), *From survival to success: Promoting minority student retention.* NASPA Monograph Series 9.

Smith, C. H. (1981). *The predominantly black college: An exploration of its role and function.* Paper presented at a meeting of the Council on Black American Affairs. ED 207 409.

Smith, D. G. (1982, Spring). The next step beyond student development: Becoming partners within our institutions. *NASPA Journal, 19,* 53–62.

Smith, D. G. (1983). Instruction and outcome in an undergraduate setting. In C. Ellner and C. Barnes (Eds.), *Studies of college teaching.* Lexington, MA: Lexington Books.

Smith, D. G. (1988). A window of opportunity for intrainstitutional collaboration. *NASPA Journal, 26*(1), 8–13.

Smith, D. H. (1980). *Admission and retention problems of black students at predominantly white universities.* Washington, DC: National Advisory Commission on Black Higher Education. ED 201 255.

Soldier, N. (1982). The adult learner in transition: The college students' changing profiles. *Journal of College Admissions, 27*(1), 24–26.

Spaights, E., Dixon, H. E., and Nicholas, S. (1985). Racism in higher education. *College Student Journal, 19*(1), 17–22.

Stampen, J. O., and Fenske, R. H. (1988). The impact of financial aid on ethnic minorities. *Review of Higher Education, 11*(4), 337–353.

Stanford Observer. (April 1989). Stanford University.

Stern, J. D. (Ed.). (1988). *The condition of education.* Washington, DC: Center for Education Statistics. ED 294 333.

Stewart, D. M. (1988). Overcoming the barriers to successful participation by minorities. *Review of Higher Education, 11*(4), 329–336.

Stilwell, D. N., Stilwell, W. E., and Perril, L. C. (1983). Barriers in higher education for persons with handicaps: A followup. *Journal of College Student Personnel, 24,* 337–343.

Stimpson, C. (1987). New consciousness, old institutions, and the need for reconciliation. In C. Lasser (Ed.), *Educating men and women together.* Urbana: University of Illinois Press.

Stoecker, J., Pascarella, E. T., and Wolfe, L. M. (1988). Persistence in higher education: A nine-year test of a theoretical model. *Journal of College Student Development, 29,* 196–209.

Sudarkasa, N. (1987). Affirmative action or affirmation of the status quo? *AAHE Bulletin, 39*(6), 3–6.

Sue, D. W. (1979). Ethnic identity: The impact of two cultures on the psychological development of Asians in America. In D. R. Atkinson, G. Morten, and D. W. Sue (Eds.), *Counseling American minorities.* Dubuque, Iowa: W.C. Brown.

Sue, D. W. (1981). *Counseling the culturally different.* New York: Wiley.

Sue, D. W. (Ed.). (1977). Counseling the culturally different. *Personnel and Guidance Journal, 55*(7).

Suen, H. K. (1983). Alienation and attrition of black students on a predominantly white campus. *Journal of College Student Personnel, 24*(2), 117–121.

Suzuki, R. H. (1984). *Socioeconomic cultural pluralism: Its meaning for the future and education.* Proceedings of the Conference on Educational and Societal Futures, April 28, 1983, Anaheim, CA.

Switkin, L. R., and Gynther, M. D. (1974). Trust, activism, and interpersonal perception in black and white college students. *Journal of Social Psychology, 94,* 153–154.

Tajfel, H. (1982). Social psychology of intergroup relations. *Annual Review of Psychology, 33,* 1–39.

Terry, R. (1981). The negative impact on white values. In B. P. Bowser and R. G. Hunt (Eds.), *Impacts of racism on white America.* Beverly Hills, CA: Sage.

Thomas, G. E. (1981). The effects of standardized achievement test performance and family status on black-white college access. In G. E. Thomas (Ed.), *Black students in higher education.* Westport, CT: Greenwood Press.

Tidball, M. E. (1973). Perspective on academic women and affirmative action. *Educational Record, 54,* 130–135.

Tidball, M. E. (1976). Of men and research: The dominant themes in American higher education include neither teaching nor women. *Journal of Higher Education, 47*(4), 373–389.

Tidball, M. E. (1980). Women's colleges and women achievers revisited. *Signs: Journal of Women in Culture and Society, 5*(3), 504–517.

Tidball, M. E. (1988). Women's colleges and women achievers revisited. In E. Minnich, J. O'Barr, and R. Rosenfeld (Eds.), *Reconstructing the academy: Women's education and women's studies.* Chicago: University of Chicago Press.

Tinto, V. (1987). *Leaving college.* Chicago: University of Chicago Press.

Tracey, T., and Sedlacek, W. (1984). Noncognitive variables in predicting academic success by race. *Measurement and Evaluation in Guidance, 16,* 171–178.

Tracey, T., and Sedlacek, W. (1985). The relationship of noncognitive variables to academic success: A longitudinal comparison by race. *Journal of College Student Personnel, 26*(5), 405–410.

Trent, W. (1984). Equity considerations in higher education: Race and sex differences in degree attainment and major field from 1976 through 1981. *American Journal of Education, 92,* 280–305.

Trent, W. T., and Braddock, J. H. (1988). Trends in black enrollment and degree attainment. In J. B. Williams, III (Ed.), *Desegregating America's colleges and universities.* New York: Teachers College Press.

Turner, C.S.V. (1987, April). *Organizational determinants of the transfer of Hispanic students from two- to four-year colleges.* Paper presented at a meeting of the American Educational Research Association, Washington, DC.

Uncapher, B. W., and Associates (1983). *Meeting needs of adult university students: A model designed by adult students.* University Park: Pennsylvania State University. ED 235 735.

U.S. Department of Commerce. (1987). *Current population reports: Educational attainment in the U.S., March 1982 to 1985.* Series P-20, No. 415. Washington, DC: U.S. Department of Commerce.

Valencia Community College. (1981). *Staff and program development: Black student retention, 1980–81.* ED 226 773.

Valverde, L. (1988). The missing element: Hispanics at the top in higher education. *Change, 20*(3), 11.

Vasquez, M.J.T. (1982). Confronting barriers to the participation of Mexican American women in higher education. *Hispanic Journal of Behavioral Sciences, 4*(2), 147–165.

Vaz, K. (1987). Building retention systems for talented minority students attending white universities. *Negro Educational Review, 38*(1), 23–29.

Verdugo, R. R. (1986). Educational stratification and Hispanics. In M. A. Olivas (Ed.), *Latino college students.* New York: Teachers College Press.

Walton, J. (1986, April). Can you really be both? Some thoughts on the education of women. *AAHE Bulletin,* 11–15.

Watson, A. (1980). *An analysis of the concept of cultural pluralism.* Doctoral dissertation, Claremont Graduate School.

Webster, D. S. (1984). Chicano students in American higher education. *Integrated Education, 22*(1), 42–51.

Weick, K. (1976). Educational organizations as loosely coupled systems. *Administrative Science Quarterly, 21*(1), 1–19.

Weick, K. (1979). *The social psychology of organizing.* New York: Random House.

Weinberg, M. (1982). In and about the campus. *Integrated Education, 20*(3–5), 3–44.

White, T. J., and Sedlacek, W. E. (1987). White Student attitudes toward blacks and Hispanics: Programming implications. *Journal of Multicultural Counseling and Development, 18*(4), 171–183.

WICHE (Western Interstate Commission on Higher Education). (1987). *From minority to majority: Education—The future of the southwest.* Boulder, CO: Author.

Wilkerson, M. B. (1987). How equal is equal education? Race, class, and gender. In C. Lasser (Ed.), *Educating men and women together: Coeducation in a changing world.* Champaign: University of Illinois Press.

Wilkerson, M. B. (1989). Majority, minority, and the numbers game. In C. S. Pearson, D. L. Shavlik, and J. G. Touchton (Eds.), *Educating the majority: Women challenge tradition in higher education.* New York: Macmillan.

Williams, J. H., and Muehl, S. (1978). Relations among student and teacher perceptions of behavior. *Journal of Negro Education, 47,* 328–336.

Willie, C. V. (1981). *The ivory and ebony towers: Race relations and higher education.* Lexington, MA: Lexington Books.

Willie, C. V., and Edmonds, R. R. (1978). *Black colleges in America.* New York: Teachers College Press.

Willie, C. V., and McCord, A. S. (1972). *Black students at white colleges.* New York: Praeger Press.

Wilson, K. M. (1980). The performance of minority students beyond freshman year: Testing a 'late-bloomer' hypothesis in one state university setting. *Research in Higher Education, 13,* 23–47.

Wilson, R. (1987a). *Minorities in higher education.* Washington, DC: American Council on Education. ED 299 844.

Wilson, R. (1987b). Recruitment and retention of minority faculty and staff. *AAHE Bulletin, 39*(6), 11–14.

Wilson, R. (1988). *Minorities in higher education.* Washington, DC: American Council on Education.

Women's College Coalition. (1981). *A study of the learning environment at women's colleges.* Washington, DC: Women's College Coalition.

Wright, D. J. (Ed.). (1987). *Responding to the needs of today's minority students.* New Directions for Student Services, No. 38. San Francisco: Jossey-Bass.

Wright, D. J., Butler, A., Switzer, V. A., and Masters, J. G. (1988). The future of minority retention. In M. C. Terrell and D. J. Wright (Eds.), *From survival to success.* NASPA Monograph Series 9.

Wright, J. J. (1984). Black higher education in the eighties. *Educational Research, 62*(3), 54–57.

Yuker, H. E., Block, J. R., and Young, J. H. (1966). *The measurement of attitudes toward disabled persons.* Albertson, NY: Human Resources Center.

Zambrana, R. E. (1987). *A profile of Chicana women in higher education: Institutional barriers.* Working paper. Los Angeles: UCLA.

Zuber, P. (1981). Moral and ethical obligations for colleges and universities to minority students. *Professional ethics in university administration.* New Directions for Higher Education, No. 33. San Francisco: Jossey-Bass.

Name Index

Burciaga, C. P., 23
Burgos-Sasscer, R., xlv
Burrell, L. F., xlii, 14, 22
Busenberg, B., xxii
Bush, J., xi
Butler, A, 22

C

Callan, P. M., 66
Capitanio, J. P., xviii
Cardoza, J., 11, 39
Carnevale, A. P., xii
Carodo, T. J., 40–41
Carter, D., xlv
Carter, R. T., 12–13, 16
Carver, C. S., 16
Castaneda, A., 29, 31
Chacon, M. A., 9, 12, 14, 23
Chambers, A., 14, 15, 40, 41
Chang, M., xi, xxi
Chew, C. A., 3, 15
Clark, B. R., 31
Claxton, C. S., 14, 16
Clayton-Pedersen, A. R., xvi
Clewell, B., 40–41, 45
Clinchy, B. M., 14, 27, 54
Cloete, N., xii–xiii
Clowes, D. A., 6
Clyde-Snyder, M., 3
Cohen, A. M., 66
Cohen, E. G., 9, 12, 14, 23
Collins, J., 20
Cope, R. G., 21
Cornewell, G. H., xiii
Courage, R., 17
Cox, T. H., Jr., xii
Cox, W. E., 9
Coyle, S., 60
Creange, R., 17, 25
Creedon, C. F., 21
Cross, K. P., 43
Cross, M., xii–xiii
Crosson, P. H., 15, 16, 17

D

Darder, A., xxviii
Dares-Hobbs, S., 20
Davenport, T., xlii, 12, 13, 29, 40, 41, 44, 58

Davis, J. E., 12
de la Teja, M. H., 15
de la Tones, A., 19
de los Santos, A. G., 4, 9, 11, 12, 39, 40, 45
Demetrulias, D. A., 18
Desjardins, C., 29
Dey, E. L., xx
DiCesare, A., 22
Dinka, F., 16
Dix, L. S., 8
Dixon, H. E., 40–41
Doane, A. W., xxviii
Donne, J., 87
Donovan, R. A., 66
Duffy, Y., xlvi–xlvii
Duhon, R. M., 17
Duran, R. P., 57, 58
Durnell, P. L., 17

E

Edelman, J. M., xlviii
Edmonds, R. R., xlviii
Ekong, D., xii–xiii
Elam, J. C., 14
El-Khawas, E., 5, 9
Engberg, M. E., xvi, xx
Epps, E. G., 11, 27, 33, 43, 44
Espiritu, Y. L., xvii
Estrada, L. F., 8
Etcheverry, R., 4
Etzioni, A., 20

F

Farren, P. J., 39
Feldman, K. A., 37
Fenderson, D. A., 18
Fenske, R. H., 4, 66, 67
Fichten, C. S., 3, 8
Ficklen, M. S., 40, 45
Fields, C., 22
Fiske, E. B., 15
Fleming, J., 11, 27, 43, 44
Ford, J. K., 34
Forer, B., 66
Fox, R. N., 25
Frable, D.E.S., xxviii
Frances, C., xli
Frankel, L., xx

Frazier, E. F., xliii
Freedman, T., 14
Fries, J. E., 5

G

Gamson, Z. F., 55, 57, 58
Gandara, P., xvi
Garcia, M., xiii, xxxi, xxxii
Garrison, R., xlii, 12–14, 29, 40, 41, 58
Garza, R. T., 15, 16
Gattiker, U. E., 40, 41
Gillespie, B., 44
Gittell, M., 39–41
Glass, D. C., 16
Glennen, R. E., 39
Goldberg, B., 40, 41
Goldberger, N., 14, 27, 54
Gordon, M., 29
Gosman, E. J., 11, 12, 15
Graham, L. P., 18
Green, K., 3
Green, M., 43, 55, 56, 64
Grieger, I., 14
Griffith, A. R., 12–13
Grubb, H. J., 58
Guarasci, R., xiii
Gudeman, R. H., xx
Guiner, L., xxviii
Gurin, G., 15
Gurin, P., xx, 11, 27, 43, 44
Gutek, B. A., 32, 34, 40, 41
Guyette, S., 11
Gynther, M. D., 16

H

Hakura, K., xi
Hall, E. R., 20
Hall, R. M., 13, 27
Hameister, B., 8
Hanch, W. E., 15
Hannah, W., 21
Harper, A., xii–xiii
Harris, J., 53
Harris, L. J., 15
Hart, P. S., 11, 12, 43
Hartnett, R. I., 11
Hemmings, A., 41
Herek, G. M., xviii

Heth, C., 11
Hetherinton, C., 17, 25
Hill, S. T., xlv, 4, 9–12
Hilton, T., 10, 11
Hinkle, D. E., 6
Hodgkinson, H., xli, 8
hooks, b., xxviii
Hope, R. O., xvi
Hrabowski, F. A., xvi
Hsia, J., xlvi, 3, 4, 14
Hu, M., 17, 25, 40, 41
Hudgins, C. A., xiii, xxxi, xxxii
Hudson, G., 18, 25
Hughes, R., xlv
Hunt, C. L., 29, 30
Hunt, R. G., 20
Hurtado, S., xvi, xx

I

Ibarra, R. A., xxviii
Inidresan, J., xii–xiii
Iovacchini, E. V., 5
Ivey, Y. A., 20

J

Jaimes, M. A., 15
Jaramillo, M. L., xlii, xlviii
Jarrow, J. E., xlvii, 5
Jobe, C. C., 9
Johansen, M. K., 17
Johnson, D. W., 33
Johnson, J. R., 25
Johnson, R. T., 33
Jones, C. J., 15
Jones, J., xi
Jones, W. T., 55

K

Kanter, R. M., 34
Katz, I., 16
Katz, J. H., 20
Kim, D., xxi
Kirchner, C., 3
Knowles, M., 17
Konrad, A. M., 32, 34
Korn, W., 3
Korolewicz, A., 16
Korolewicz, M., 16

P

Pace, C. R., 22, 27
Padilla, F. M., xxviii
Palmer, P. J, 27, 53
Pantages, T. J., 21
Parker, W. M., 14, 15, 40, 41
Pascarella, E. T., xviii–xix, 11, 12, 25–27, 44
Patterson, A. M., 12–14, 18
Pearson, C. S., xlii, xlv, 14, 17, 23, 40, 41, 46, 47, 54
Perril, L. C., 18
Perry, D. C., 3, 5
Perry, F. W., 14
Peterson, M. W., 12–15, 29, 40, 41, 55, 57, 58, xlii
Pettigrew, T. F., xlii, xlvii, xx, 1, 31
Pfeffer, J., 34
Pilant, D. E., 16
Polkington, D. E., xxxii
Ponjuan, L., xvi, xx
Ponterotto, J. G., 14
Pounds, A. W., xliv

Q

Quevedo-Garcia, E. L., 29

R

Rasor, M., 14
Rendón, L. I., xvi, 40, 57
Rice, J. K., 41
Richardson, R. C., Jr., 6, 11–13, 18, 39, 40, 45, 55, 57, 59, 66
Robison, G., 12–14
Rochin, R., 19
Rodriguez, M., 14
Rokeach, M., 29
Rolison, G., 26, 34
Rooks, C. J., 16
Rooney, G. D., 25
Rosen, N. L., xlv, 4
Rosener, J. B., xii
Rossi, A., 14
Rotermund, M. K., 4
Roueche, J. E., 40–41

S

Salganik, L. H., xlv
Sanders, D., 11, 14–16, 27
Sandler, B. R., 13, 14, 27, 34
Saslow, R. S., 17
Sattler, J. L., 18
Scales, W. R., 18
Schaier-Peleg, B., 66
Schmidt, M. R., xlv
Schoem, D., xx
Schuster, J., 60
Scott, J., 14, 15, 40, 41
Sedlacek, W. E., xiii, xlvii, xviii, xxxi, xxxii, 4, 8, 12–16, 18, 22, 23, 58
Seeman, M., 19
Shavlik, D. L., xlii, xlv, 14, 17, 23, 40, 41, 45, 47, 54
Silverstein, J., 53
Simmons, H., 9, 11, 12, 42, 45
Simon, Z., 3
Skinner, E. F., 13, 55, 57
Slaughter, J. B., 56
Smart, J. C., xviii–xix, 6, 44
Smith, C. H., 43
Smith, D. G., xiii, xix, xvi, xx, xxii, xxiv, xxix, xxxi, xxxii, 53, 60, 65
Smith D. H., 51
Soldier, N., 17, 40, 41
Solorzano, D. G., xxviii
Spaights, E., 40–41
Sprandel, H. Z., xlv
Stampen, J. O., 4, 66, 67
Steele, C., xvi
Stern J. D., 8
Stewart, D. M., 57
Stewart, M. A., 5, 16
Stilwell, D. N., 18
Stilwell, W. E., 18
Stimpson, C., 42
Stoecker, J., xviii–xix, 26, 44
Strover, S., 9, 12, 14, 23
Sudarkasa, N., 11, 52
Sue, D. W., xlvi, xlvii, 14–15, 29
Suen, H. K., 14, 15, 23
Suzuki, R. H., 30
Switkin, L. R., 16
Switzer, V. A., 22

T

Tajfel, H., 32, 33
Tarule, J. M., 14, 27, 54
Tatum, B. D., xix

Subject Index

A

Academic engagement, xxi
Academic integration, 26
Academic preparation, 22–24
Access
   versus quality, 57–60
   and success, xiii–xviii
ACE, 43, 46
Administrative practices, 71
Adult learner, 17
Alienation, 28
American Council on Education, xliii
American Dilemma, An (Myrdal), xliii
Asian American, xlv
Asian American Student Foundation, 4
Assessment, institutional, 63–64
Assimilation, 29
Audit, institutional, 63–64

B

Background characteristics, role of, 20–24

C

California, x, xii, 65
   Proposition 209, x
and community colleges, 8
Campus environment, 12–13
Carnegie Commission for the Advancement
   of Teaching, 14
Carnegie Foundation, xxix, 3, 4, 8
Center for Education Statistics, x, 2, 3,
   5, 6
Class, xvii

Climate
   campus, xviii–xx
   current status of, xxv–xxvii
Commission on Minority Participation, xliii,
   1, 8, 10, 11, 40
Commitment, 66–67
Competition, 27, 52
Conflict, dealing with, xxx–xxxi, 55–56
Cooperation, competition *versus,* 52
Cooperative Institutional Research Project
   database, 10
Cost, 66–67
Council of Graduate Schools, 11,
   64, 66
Cultural pluralism, xxvii–xxviii, 29–31
Curriculum, 70

D

Demography, xxvii–xxviii, 33–35, 60
Disabled students, 17–18
Diversity
   context for, outside of higher education,
      x–xxiv
   educating for, xxx, 56–57
   on faculty and staff, 50–52
   fundamental issues of organizing for,
      xxix–xxxii, 49–61
   implications of, 45–47
   institutional responses to, 39–47
   status of, 1–20
   summary, 45
   value of, 31

About the Authors

Daryl G. Smith is professor of education and psychology at Claremont Graduate University in Claremont, California. Her research interests center on diversity in higher education, evaluation and organizational change, college governance issues, women in academe, women's colleges, institutional research, student affairs, and classroom teaching.

Lisa E. Wolf-Wendel is associate professor of higher education at the University of Kansas in Lawrence. Her research focuses broadly on equity issues concerning women and people of color in higher education. Lisa earned her doctorate in higher education from the Claremont Graduate School, where Daryl Smith was her major advisor.

About the ASHE Higher Education Reports Series

Since 1983, the ASHE (formerly ASHE-ERIC) Higher Education Report Series has been providing researchers, scholars, and practitioners with timely and substantive information on the critical issues facing higher education. Each monograph presents a definitive analysis of a higher education problem or issue, based on a thorough synthesis of significant literature and institutional experiences. Topics range from planning to diversity and multiculturalism, to performance indicators, to curricular innovations. The mission of the Series is to link the best of higher education research and practice to inform decision making and policy. The reports connect conventional wisdom with research and are designed to help busy individuals keep up with the higher education literature. Authors are scholars and practitioners in the academic community. Each report includes an executive summary, review of the pertinent literature, descriptions of effective educational practices, and a summary of key issues to keep in mind to improve educational policies and practice.

The Series is one of the most peer reviewed in higher education. A National Advisory Board made up of ASHE members reviews proposals. A National Review Board of ASHE scholars and practitioners reviews completed manuscripts. Six monographs are published each year and they are approximately 120 pages in length. The reports are widely disseminated through Jossey-Bass and John Wiley & Sons, and they are available online to subscribing institutions through Wiley InterScience (http://www.interscience.wiley.com).

Call for Proposals

The ASHE Higher Education Report Series is actively looking for proposals. We encourage you to contact one of the editors, Dr. Kelly Ward (kaward@wsu.edu) or Dr. Lisa Wolf-Wendel (lwolf@ku.edu), with your ideas.

Recent Titles

Back Issue/Subscription Order Form

Copy or detach and send to:
Jossey-Bass, A Wiley Imprint, 989 Market Street, San Francisco CA 94103-1741

Call or fax toll-free: Phone 888-378-2537 6:30AM – 3PM PST; Fax 888-481-2665

Back Issues: Please send me the following issues at $24 each
(Important: please include series abbreviation and issue number.
For example AEHE 28:1)

_____

_____

_____

$ _____   **Total for single issues**

$ _____   SHIPPING CHARGES: SURFACE   Domestic Canadian

		First Item	$5.00	$6.00
		Each Add'l Item	$3.00	$1.50

For next-day and second-day delivery rates, call the number listed above

Subscriptions   Please ❑ start ❑ renew my subscription to _ASHE-ERIC Higher
Education Reports_ for the year 2_____ at the following rate:

U.S.	❑ Individual $165	❑ Institutional $175
Canada	❑ Individual $165	❑ Institutional $235
All Others	❑ Individual $213	❑ Institutional $286

❑ Online subscriptions available too!

**For more information about online subscriptions visit
www.interscience.wiley.com**

$ _____   Total single issues and subscriptions (Add appropriate sales tax
for your state for single issue orders. No sales tax for U.S.
subscriptions. Canadian residents, add GST for subscriptions and
single issues.)

❑ Payment enclosed (U.S. check or money order only)
❑ VISA ❑ MC ❑ AmEx ❑ #_____ Exp. Date _____

Signature _____ Day Phone _____
❑ Bill Me (U.S. institutional orders only. Purchase order required.)

Purchase order # _____
    Federal Tax ID13559302   GST 89102 8052

Name _____

Address _____

_____

Phone _____ E-mail _____

For more information about Jossey-Bass, visit our Web site at **www.josseybass.com**

ASHE-ERIC HIGHER EDUCATION REPORT IS NOW AVAILABLE ONLINE AT WILEY INTERSCIENCE

What is Wiley InterScience?

Wiley InterScience is the dynamic online content service from John Wiley & Sons delivering the full text of over 300 leading scientific, technical, medical, and professional journals, plus major reference works, the acclaimed Current Protocols laboratory manuals, and even the full text of select Wiley print books online.

What are some special features of Wiley InterScience?

Wiley Interscience Alerts is a service that delivers table of contents via e-mail for any journal available on Wiley InterScience as soon as a new issue is published online.
Early View is Wiley's exclusive service presenting individual articles online as soon as they are ready, even before the release of the compiled print issue. These articles are complete, peer-reviewed, and citable.
CrossRef is the innovative multi-publisher reference linking system enabling readers to move seamlessly from a reference in a journal article to the cited publication, typically located on a different server and published by a different publisher.

How can I access Wiley InterScience?

Visit http://www.interscience.wiley.com.

Guest Users can browse Wiley InterScience for unrestricted access to journal Tables of Contents and Article Abstracts, or use the powerful search engine.
Registered Users are provided with a *Personal Home Page* to store and manage customized alerts, searches, and links to favorite journals and articles. Additionally, Registered Users can view free Online Sample Issues and preview selected material from major reference works.
Licensed Customers are entitled to access full-text journal articles in PDF, with select journals also offering full-text HTML.

How do I become an Authorized User?

Authorized Users are individuals authorized by a paying Customer to have access to the journals in Wiley InterScience. For example, a University that subscribes to Wiley journals is considered to be the Customer.
Faculty, staff and students authorized by the University to have access to those journals in Wiley InterScience are Authorized Users. Users should contact their Library for information on which Wiley journals they have access to in Wiley InterScience.

ASK YOUR INSTITUTION ABOUT WILEY INTERSCIENCE TODAY!